POLYCHROMATIC
SCREEN PRINTING

POLYCHROMATIC SCREEN PRINTING

Joy Stocksdale

ACKNOWLEDGEMENTS

I would like to thank all the marvelous people who contributed to this book. I am grateful to Judith Dern, Catherine Taylor, Nan Beaty Stocksdale, Charlie Sweet, Douglas Payne, and Michele and Eric Mills, all of whom edited or typed the manuscript. I greatly appreciate the advice, criticism, information, and support of all the reviewers: Dana Turner, Jackie Wollenberg, Nicholas Pinette, Kathleen Larisch, Michael Katz, Michael Flynn, Anne Lipow, and Don Blake. Augusta Andrea Lucas did wonderful illustrations for which I am grateful. Special thanks to Charles Frizzell for the front cover photo, Cathy Nyhan for the back cover photo, and Dana Turner for the photos which appear within the book. Without Malcolm Margolin, whom I enlisted for some neighborly help, this book would not exist. He has seriously and humorously guided me through many aspects of publishing to bring this book into the world.

Cover photo: Polychromatic wallhanging by Joy Stocksdale
Photo by Charles Frizzell

Published by Oregon Street Press
2145 Oregon Street, Berkeley, California 94705

Typesetting and design by Heyday Books
Printed and bound by Edwards Brothers, Ann Arbor, Michigan

10   9   8   7   6   5   4   3   2

Table of Contents

Introduction 1

How to Use This Book and Advice to the Beginner 2

Illustrations of Steps in Polychromatic Printing 3

1   Summary of Steps in Polychromatic Printing 5

2   Complete List of Materials 8

3   Print Screen Construction and Squeegee Size 10
    Materials, Calculating Screen Size, Frame Construction,
    Stretching the Screen, Permanent Frame, Squeegee Size,
    Discussion

4   Print Surface 19
    Materials, Size of Print Board, Directions, Discussion

5   Where to Print 25

6   Work Space Arrangement and Process Organization 26

7   Well Calculations and Tracing Design on Screen 27
    Materials, Well Size, Tracing Design on Screen, Discussion

8   Resist 33
    Materials, Recipe, Application, Discussion

9   Dye Procedures 40
    Materials, Recipe, Application, Clearing Blocked Areas
    on Screen, Discussion

10 Masking the Screen for Wells 50
    Materials, Directions for Temporary Wells,
    Permanent Masked Wells

11 Print Paste 54
    Materials, Recipe, Discussion

12 Fabric Sequence for Printing and Fabric Characteristics 59
    Guidelines for Fabric Sequence, Fabric Categories,
    Chart for Fabric Sequence, Discussion

13   Stretching the Print Fabric 66
      Materials, Directions, Discussion

14   Pulling Prints 69
      Materials, Directions, Discussion

15   Batching 75
      Materials, Directions, Discussion

16   Washing Off 80
      Materials, Directions

17   Printing on Paper 82
      Materials, Directions, Discussion

18   Cleaning After Printing 85
      Materials, Directions

19   Care of Printing Equipment 87

20   Problems and Solutions 89

21   Other Ideas for Polychromatic Printing 96

      Conclusion 99

      APPENDIX A   Where to Buy Materials 101

      APPENDIX B   Complete List of Recipes 105

      APPENDIX C   Silk Organza and Cotton Organdy Print Screen ... 106

      APPENDIX D   Bath Dyeing 107
          Materials, Recipe, Directions, Test Color of Dye Bath,
          Receptivity of Fabric to Dye, Where to Dye, Discussion

      APPENDIX E   Color Mixing 114

      APPENDIX F   Bath Dyeing in the Washing Machine 116

      GLOSSARY 118

      INDEX 122

ILLUSTRATIONS

Stretching the Print Screen 14
Print Screen and Squeegee 15
Print Board 22
Design Formats 29
Application of Resist 36
Temporary Wells 52
Taping the Print Fabric 67
Positioning Screen on Print Fabric 71
Pulling Print 72
Batching Prints 76-77

PHOTOGRAPHS

Illustrations of Steps in Polychromatic Printing 3
Filling Tjanting Reservoir with Resist 35
Painting Dye on Print Screen 42
Dye Blocking the Screen Mesh 44

Introduction

This book is about a new textile printing process—one that offers direct use and fewer steps, enabling a spontaneous approach, in contrast to the planning and many stages required in traditional screen printing methods. For the last fifteen years, I have been exploring different aspects of textile design. My work has included all types of needlework, weaving, painting and printing on fabric.

In 1978, I spent a year in England, studying textiles at Goldsmith's College of the University of London. During that time, I was introduced to a textile screen printing process which produced a multicolored monoprint. I was able to adapt this process to paper also.

Upon my return to the United States, I developed a polychromatic printing method based on the monoprint technique I learned while in England. Expanding the original concept enabled me to obtain a limited edition of five to eight prints from a single prepared screen. At the present time, I am using the polychromatic printing method on a production basis to print silk fabric for jackets, kimonos, vests and wall hangings.

The polychromatic process simplifies screen printing on fabric or paper, because, unlike traditional screen printing, the entire image is printed at the same time, rather than in several stages, using separate screens for each color. With the polychromatic process, all the colors are painted on one screen and printed with one pull of a squeegee. One screen means fewer steps and also eliminates the concern about color registration, offering the artist more flexibility and spontaneity.

This book presents the step–by–step basics of polychromatic printing. In addition, sections have been included about bath dyeing with fiber reactive dyes, color mixing, and testing methods. The *Discussion* sections present many other resists, dyes and textile techniques which can also be used with polychromatic printing. It is my hope that this exciting method will become a widely used standard printing form. I hope other textile artists will be inspired, as I have been, by the possibilities of polychromatic printing.

How to Use This Book
and Advice to The Beginner

Polychromatic printing combines printing and fabric painting techniques in a unique method. The book contains not only the step–by–step basics for the process, but also includes possibilities for going beyond the basics. The *Discussion* sections in each chapter, which add background on technique and materials, suggest other possibilities for printing polychromatically.

The beginner might want to start by reading the "Summary of Steps in Polychromatic Printing," page 5. Choose a simple design. As an inexpensive means to experiment, use artist's stretcher bars rather than heavy wooden ones, purchase only the primary dye colors (refer to "Color Mixing," page 114), and print on paper instead of fabric.

Polychromatic printing has fewer steps and takes less time than most screen printing processes. When the process is repeated a few times, it will become simple, and the results and advantages will prove polychromatic printing an easy, exciting technique to explore—for beginners, as well as experienced printers.

Illustrations of Steps in Polychromatic Printing

1. PRINT SCREEN AND SQUEEGEE.

2. APPLYING RESIST ON SCREEN WITH TJANTING TOOL, DRY.

3. PAINTING DYE ON PRINT SCREEN, DRY.

4. PLACING STRIPS OF PAPER ON SCREEN FOR WELLS.

5. STRETCHING FABRIC ON PRINT BOARD WITH TAPE.

6. LOWERING SCREEN OVER PRINT BOARD WITH FABRIC.

7. POURING PRINT PASTE ON SCREEN IN WELL AREA.

8. PULLING SQUEEGEE WITH PRINT PASTE ACROSS SCREEN.

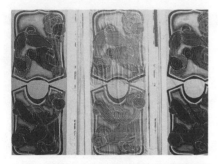

9. EACH PULL PRODUCES ONE PRINT. SUCCESSIVE PRINTS ARE LIGHTER.

10. ROLLING PRINTED FABRIC IN PLASTIC TO FIX DYE, BATCHING.

11. RINSING PRINT PASTE AND EXCESS DYE FROM PRINT FABRIC.

12. FINISHED GARMENT.

1
Summary of Steps
in Polychromatic Printing

Following is a general review of the steps involved in polychromatic printing. It is only an outline; detailed instructions for the printing process with full discussions may be found in the chapters with corresponding headings.

1. Print Screen Construction (page 10)

First in the printing process is the preparation of the print screen. This screen can be either purchased or constructed at home. If a purchased screen is used, the screen fabric may need to be replaced with another fabric more suitable to the polychromatic printing process. See page 11 for appropriate screen fabric. Choose a screen size with internal measurements at least 2″ larger than the outline of your design on top and bottom, and 1″ on each side. This border will allow wells around the design for holding the print paste and squeegee between each print pull. (See diagram, page 15.)

2. Preparation of Print Surface (page 19)

A smooth surface table, portable plywood board, or the suggested light-weight print boards may be used as a printing surface. The print surface must be slightly padded to make good contact between the screen and fabric during printing. Dacron batting makes an excellent pad. A taut plastic covering is taped or tacked over the padding so dyes and print paste may be easily washed off the printing surface.

3. Transfer of the Design to the Screen (page 27)

The design may be painted directly onto the screen, or the design cartoon may be placed beneath the screen and the design traced onto the screen with water-soluble pen or pencil. In all cases, it is important that the design be centered so that no part extends into the screen wells.

4. Mixing and Applying the Resist (page 33)
The resist is applied to the screen in desired areas to prevent dyes from bleeding and to keep the print paste from passing through the screen. A tjanting tool is used to apply the resist in a thin line, or it can be painted on in larger areas. Resist is not necessary in all situations.

5. Mixing and Painting the Dyes (page 40)
Fiber reactive dye powders are diluted with water. Dyes are then painted on the print screen within resist lines, which hold the dye in place. Dyes may also be painted outside the resist lines or painted on screens which have no resist, when bleeding is desired. Dyes must dry on the screen before printing.

6. Preparation of the Screen for Printing (page 50)
The print screen must be masked around the design area to form well for holding the print paste and squeegee. The wells are made by taping paper strips onto the screen.

7. Fabric for Printing (page 66)
For a clean print, the fabric to be printed is stretched taut over the prepared print surface and taped in place. This ensures good screen contact with all areas of the fabric.

8. Mixing the Print Paste (page 54)
The print paste is a wetting medium which is pulled across the dye-painted screen with the squeegee to release the dye onto the fabric. The print paste also carries the chemicals for fixing the dye into the fabric.

9. Pulling Prints (page 69)
Once the screen has been painted, it is placed over the stretched fabric on

the prepared printing surface. Print paste is poured along the top well and the squeegee placed in the well behind the print paste. The print paste is then pulled across the screen with the firmly held squeegee. One pull of the squeegee releases some of the dye from the screen onto the fabric below for the first print. Either the printed fabric beneath the screen is removed and a new piece of fabric on a print board is shifted into place, or the screen is moved onto a new piece of stretched fabric and the printing process is repeated. From 5 to 8 prints may be obtained from a single screen painting.

10. Batching (page 75)
The dye is fixed into the printed fabric by "batching." This is a method of fixing dye by rolling the damp printed fabric in plastic for at least 24 hours.

11. Washing Off of Printed Fabrics (page 80)
Once the fabric has been "batched," it is rinsed thoroughly in cold water. This removes the excess dye and print paste. The fabric is spin-dried or rolled in towels until it is damp-dry. It is then ironed or line-dried and is ready for final use.

2
Complete List of Materials

For more detailed information about the items listed below, refer to the materials list at the beginning of each chapter. To obtain these materials refer to "Where to Buy," Appendix A, page 101.

Print Screen and Squeegee (page 10)
artist's wooden stretcher bars or
    heavy wooden bars
sheer 100% polyester curtain fabric
staple gun
small and large hammer
corrugated fasteners
squeegee
varnish
paint brush

Print Surface (page 19)
½" - ¾" thick Dacron batting
heavy gauge plastic
corrugated cardboard
¾" thick styrofoam or rigid insulation
duct tape
scissors
water-based linoleum or carpet
    adhesive
paint roller and pan
plywood

Well Calculations and Tracing Design on Screen (page 27)
tracing paper or drawing paper
pencil or felt tip pen
water soluble pen or pencil

Resist (page 33)
Inko resist
Wilhold white glue or Sobo glue
mixing bowl
water
squeeze bottle
tjanting tool
paint brush
paper towels

Dye Procedures (page 40)
fiber reactive dyes
water
measuring spoons
small glass or plastic containers
paint brushes
rubber gloves
fine particle face mask
small stiff brush
newspapers
paper towels

Masking Screen for Wells (page 50)
For Temporary Masking
 paper or tape
For Permanent Masking
 masking compound or Proseal
 throwaway rubber gloves
 throwaway plastic mixing bowls
 throwaway paint brush
 newspaper
 masking tape
 measuring tape

Print Paste (page 54)
soda ash
urea
water
sodium alginate
two-quart plastic pitcher
blender (optional)
large mixing spoon
measuring cups

Stretching the Print Fabric (page 66)
cotton, silk, rayon or linen fabric
masking tape

Pulling Print (page 69)
waxed paper
long apron
rubber gloves

Batching (page 75)
large sheets of plastic
fine-misting spray bottle
rubber gloves

Washing Off (page 80)
rubber gloves
towels or washing machine
 (spin cycle)
tub of cold water

Printing on Paper (page 82)
print screen
resist
fiber reactive dyes
Dr. Martin's or liquid watercolors
Caran D'ache watercolor crayons
paint brush
print surface
paper
masking tape
print paste

Cleaning After Printing (page 85)
garden hose with nozzle
sponge
bucket of water

Dye Bath (page 107)
fiber reactive dyes
5-gallon plastic container
rubber gloves
timer
8 oz. container
spoon
blender
set of measuring spoons
washing machine or towels
plastic clothes pins
one pound of cotton, viscose rayon,
 silk or linen fabric
sponge
salt
soda ash

3
Print Screen Construction
And Squeegee Size

Summary

The objective is to stretch an open mesh fabric tightly over the wooden frame. This screen must be taut in order to produce clear prints.

The size of the screen varies according to the largest design and the number of prints needed. It can be reused many times and will last longest if the wood is first sealed with varnish.

The squeegee is a long, hard rubber blade in a wooden handle. It is moved down the length of the screen with firm pressure to force a thin layer of print paste through the mesh. It is important to use the correct length squeegee to fit the screen and design. The correct length is approximately 1″ shorter than the *internal* measurement of the width of the print screen.

Sections to follow: Materials; Calculating Screen Size; Frame Construction; Stretching the Screen; Permanent Frame; Squeegee Size; and Discussion.

Materials

Artist's wooden stretcher bars or heavy wooden bars. (Refer to "Calculating Frame Size," page 11, to determine bar length.) Artist's stretcher bars are for a small, temporary print frame up to 24″ square in outside dimensions. Heavy, wooden bars are needed for permanent print frames. Frame sizes near 12″ × 24″ require 1½″ × 2″ wood stock. Frame sizes 24″-36″ to 36″ × 54″ require 2″-3″ wood stock.

Fabric for screen—sheer 100% polyester curtain fabric. Purchase enough fabric to extend 4″ beyond all four sides of frame. Curtain fabric with the trade names "Finesse" or "Ninnon" can be found in most drapery departments. It has an even weave and comes in widths up to 118″.

Screen printer's polyester screening, multifilament size 8xx or 10xx, may be used as an alternative to curtain fabric. Used screens cleaned with solvents, bleach, or TSP may alter or weaken the dye colors. It is recommended to begin with a new screen or one that has been cleaned with only water. Both the screen printer's fabric and the curtain fabric may provide a permanent screen.

Staple gun. A lightweight staple gun is adequate. NOTE: a heavyweight gun for an artist's canvas can pucker screen fabrics.

Hammers. One small hammer, 10-12 oz.; one large hammer, 16-20 oz.

Corrugated fasteners. Purchase at any hardware store four 1″-long fasteners or four angle plates to stregthen corners of frame.

Squeegee. Square edge, rubber blade of medium stiffness. For squeegee size, refer to page 16.

Varnish.

Paint brush. 1″ wide for applying varnish.

Calculating Screen Size

There are two major considerations in determining frame dimensions. First, what is the largest design size desired? A screen can always be masked off to print smaller designs, but it cannot be made larger. Second, how many prints in each edition are required? The size of the screen can determine how many prints there will be in each edition. Maximum pressure must be applied to the squeegee for each print, but because larger screens require longer squeegees, and less pressure can be applied to long squeegees, an average of only 4 to 5 prints can be obtained from a screen 24″ square or larger. With smaller screens, however, the number of prints increases to about eight. More pressure can be applied to a smaller squeegee, thereby forcing less print paste and dye through the screen, so that there is more dye left for more prints.

In addition to these two considerations, the wells around the design and the thickness of the frame bars also determine the final frame size. The wells border the print or design area and are used to hold the print paste away from the design between each print pull. To calculate the wells, add 1" *on each vertical side* of the print area. On the *top and bottom* of the print area, add 2" to 3". This gives the internal measurements of the frame. To these, add the width of the stretcher bars on all four sides for the outside dimensions. This total gives the length of stretcher bars needed to fit the design size and also allows room for the wells. (Refer to diagram, page 15).

Frame Construction
Wedge corners of stretcher bars tightly together. Check to see that the joint is tightly closed. All bars must be at right angles. Check this by holding frame corner against a table corner. Reinforce corners of frame by pounding corrugated fasteners diagonally across mitered joint with a large hammer. (Refer to diagram, page 14).

Stretching the Screen
Place frame over screen fabric with the corrugated-fastener-side-up so as not to snag or cut screen fabric. Cut screen fabric at least 4" larger around all four sides of frame. This fabric border will be pulled up and over the frame edge and stapled in place. The grain of the fabric should be parallel with the frame edge. Use a selvedge edge or center fold to help align the fabric with the frame. Place the frame on a sturdy table or place it flat on the floor. At this point it is helpful to have two people working together on this step. One will stretch the screen fabric as tightly as possible, and one will staple and hammer the fabric onto the stretcher bars.

Beginning in the middle on the selvedge edge, if the fabric has one, bring the fabric up and over the back side of the frame to the center of the bar. Staple the fabric in place, keeping the staple parallel to the edge of the frame. Hammer the staple down, so it will hold the fabric tightly in place.

Continue hammering and stapling every 2″ along the bar, moving out from the center to each corner, pulling fabric firmly. Leave fabric in the corners unstapled. On the opposite side of the frame, begin in the center and pull the fabric as tightly as possible straight across to keep the grain even from side to side. Bring the fabric up and over the edge of the frame, place a staple there and hammer down. Continue, pulling the fabric straight across the frame and out slightly to each corner, staple and hammer in place. Repeat this process for the remaining two sides. The screen should be tight and should bounce when tapped with the hand.

At the corners, gather fabric together and staple the gathers to hold them in place. Trim excess fabric that is hanging in print area to inner edge of frame to keep it out of the way of printing. (Refer to diagram, page 14.)

Permanent Frame

The artist's wooden stretcher bar frame may warp or become loose. It is meant primarily as an inexpensive way of experimenting with the polychromatic technique. Frames for extensive printing should be made out of heavier wood stock. Dry cedar or pine are best because they absorb water slowly and will not warp with continual use. To ensure a minimum of water absorption, seal the surface of the wooden bars with several coats of varnish. Strengthen corners by using tongue-and-groove or half-lap joints. For additional support, a flat L-shaped angle plate may be screwed onto the back of the frame. For best results, large screens should be stretched professionally at a screen printers' supply outlet. At these outlets, heavy-duty frames can also be purchased or made to order.

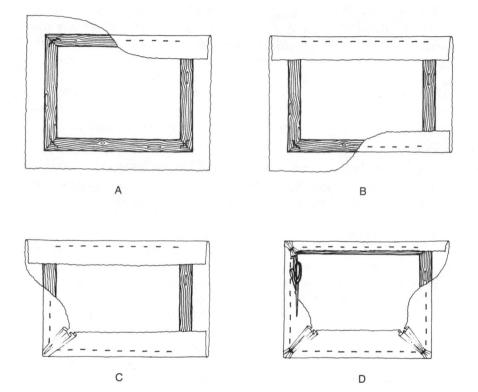

STRETCHING THE PRINT SCREEN
(A) Start in middle stapling out to corners. (B) In the center on opposite side, pulling screen fabric as tight as possible, staple out to corners. (C) Repeat step (A) on other side, pulling screen fabric slightly. (D) Repeat step (B) on remaining side. Gather fabric together in corners and staple. Trim excess fabric.

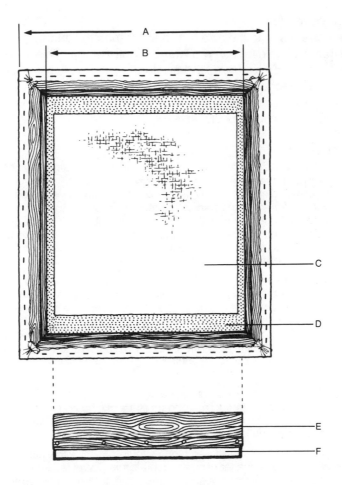

PRINT SCREEN AND SQUEEGEE
(A) external measurement of the print screen (B) internal measurement of the print screen (C) largest print area of the screen (D) the wells, measuring at least 2"-3" on top and bottom and 1" on the sides (E) handle of the squeegee (F) rubber blade of the squeege (The squeegee measures at least 1" shorter than the internal width measurement.)

Squeegee Size

The correct squeegee size is 1″ shorter than the internal measurement of the frame in the direction you intend to pull the print. This allows ½″ ease on each side. For example, if the internal frame width measures 14″, the correct squeegee size is 13″. (Refer to diagram, page 15.) A smaller squeegee can be used if your design does not take up the whole print area. The squeegee must extend at least ½″ into the wells on the sides.

Discussion

Artist's wooden stretcher bars are suggested for a small, inexpensive, temporary print frame. Over time, the narrow bars will warp from screen tension and repeated cleaning with water. Therefore, heavy wooden bars, painted with varnish for water resistance, are recommended for permanent print screens. Also available are metal frames with screw bars for applying tension on the screen. Some metal frames allow any number of screens to be removed, stored, and replaced in perfect registration. This cuts down on having to buy new frames to save an image.

There are several methods for stretching a screen on the frame. The heavy, wooden bars manufactured for screen printing often have a groove for cording. The screening is placed over the grooved side of the frame. The cord is forced into the groove by hammering on a thin piece of metal, such as a door hinge. Hammer the cord in, moving in a circular direction around the frame, pulling the screen tight. This is usually a good way to obtain very tight tension. If the screen is loose, the printed image will have blurry edges and the screen will be harder to clean.

Stapling the screen is a quick method for small temporary frames. Sometimes stapling is done through cardboard strips or a heavy fabric tape. This prevents the staples from embedding in the wood and becoming difficult to remove. The tape can be pulled up together with the staples.

Whether or not the screen fabric should be wet with water before stretching seems to be a matter of personal preference. Wet fabric will not shift as much as slippery, dry fabric during frame stretching. Silk should be wet, because the fiber stretches slightly, but stretching is minimal with polyester. Using dry fabric, on the other hand, saves the steps of wetting and drying fabric. Also, some people find dry fabric easier to handle.

Screen Fabrics

Polyester screen fabric is most commonly used by printers. It is less expensive than silk mesh, more durable, and stretches less when wet. Nylon can stretch and blur the image. Silk was the first mesh used in screen printing, but the advantages of polyester have made silk less prevalent. There is a slight roughness, or tooth, to silk, which makes it a better choice when the design stencil or blocking agent will not adhere to polyester.

Polyester curtain fabric is a good choice for polychromatic printing either for permanent or temporary screens. It is inexpensive compared to traditional screen print mesh and will retain no afterimage from dye left in the fibers. An afterimage left in the screen after cleaning can be confusing when the printer applies a new design on the screen. Traditional silk-screen fabric will hold a dark afterimage, because fiber reactive dyes used in the polychromatic process fix on silk. Using bleach to remove the dye will weaken silk fibers. Refer to Appendix C, page 106, for using silk organza and cotton organdy.

Different sizes of screen mesh are available. The larger mesh (called by the smaller xx number) does not give so much detailing and resolution as a finer mesh. But the smaller mesh does not allow so much print paste or ink to pass through and may have to be squeegeed a few times to leave an adequate deposit. Screens between 8xx and 16xx are used by most textile printers to obtain a sufficient deposit on a slightly textured fabric surface. Paper may be less textured and is often smoother, so a finer mesh can be used.

For polychromatic printing, the large mesh screen allows the maximum amount of dye to be painted on the screen, without the dye, when dry, blocking the mesh. The large mesh also permits enough print paste to pass through with one pull of the squeegee. Finer mesh screens can be used, but there may be more dye blockage, and more than one pass of the squeegee may be needed to obtain a clear print.

Squeegee

Soft, medium, and hard grades of stiffness are available in squeegee blades. When choosing a blade, consider the texture of the surface to be printed (usually fabric or paper), the amount of deposit needed, and the screen mesh size. If the surface to be printed is textured, use a soft blade that will conform. For smooth or slightly textured surfaces, medium to hard blades are appropriate. For more deposit, use a soft blade. Medium blades, overall, are most widely used.

Blades are available in a variety of edges. Most textile printers use a rounded or square edge. A rounded edge leaves more deposit than a square one. Rubber or polyurethane composition (plastic) are the most common blades. Rubber does not keep a sharp edge as long as polyurethane does, but rubber is less expensive.

In most screen printing, the squeegee can be pulled several times over the screen without harming the print. But if the full potential of the polychromatic process is to be reached, good contact, releasing the least possible amounts of dye from the screen with each pull of the squeegee, is necessary. A square-edged, medium-stiff blade is recommended. A rounded-edged blade deposits too much print paste and dye—and a hard, stiff blade, not enough. A soft blade will blend under pressure and deposit too much print paste and dye. Refer to "Pulling of the Print," page 73, for further considerations.

4

Print Surface

Summary

The objective is to construct an absolutely flat, smooth, slightly padded surface to provide even contact between the screen and fabric in order to produce a clear print.

Various types of padding materials may be used. A taut plastic covering is then placed over the padded surface, so that the dyes and print paste may be easily washed off. This padded, plastic surface may be constructed over an existing table top or plywood board. An alternative lightweight foundation board can also be made using styrofoam covered with corrugated cardboard, then covered with padding and plastic. The following directions are for constructing the lightweight print board.

Sections to follow: Materials; Size of Print Board; Directions; and Discussion.

Materials

½" to ¾" *thick Dacron batting.* Purchase by the yard to cover top of board for padding. NOTE: If you have a large print board, batting can be seamed to fit. Refer to directions, page 21. Layers of smooth blankets or felt, rug felting, or ¼" thick firm foam rubber can also be used, but they should not be uneven, folded or textured.

12 to 16 gauge heavy plastic or oilcloth. Do not use a textured or plastic surface that might show through onto print. Plastic must be long and wide enough to wrap around the back of print board and must have no seams which will show when printing.

Corrugated cardboard. Two pieces can be seamed carefully to fit top and bottom of the styrofoam board if absolutely necessary. It is best if the cardboard is wide enough to make seaming unnecessary.

¾" thick styrofoam or rigid insulation. Same size as the corrugated cardboard. NOTE: If necessary, piece in opposite direction of cardboard seams.

Duct tape. 4" wide tape is better than 3".

Scissors. For cutting plastic and padding.

Water-based linoleum or carpet adhesive. CAUTION: Some solvent base adhesives will melt styrofoam.

Paint roller and pan. To be used to roll the adhesive onto the styrofoam and cardboard surfaces.

Plywood. ¼" or thicker, one piece the approximate size of the print board.

Size of Print Board

To give the print board support, lay it on a work table. The board will be stiff, so it can be slightly larger than the table it is placed on, as long as it does not tip when pressure is applied in printing.

For small screens: Several prints can be made upon one large piece of stretched fabric on one print board, or several smaller pieces of fabric can be taped to one board. The four sides of the print screen frame must be supported for at least ½" by the board. If printing several pieces of fabric on one board, arrange enough space around each fabric piece so that the frame does not overlap other prints. Refer to diagram, page 71. If the frame must overlap a wet print, place waxed paper over the printed fabric to protect it.

For large screens: The print board can be as large as the screen frame. The one piece of stretched fabric on a print board can be aligned with the print area of the screen. One board per print is needed. Usually, five prints can be made from a big screen, so five boards are needed. The board must be large enough to overlap at least ½" onto the wooden bars of the screen frame. Refer to diagram, page 71.

Directions

Cut corrugated cardboard and styrofoam the exact size of the print board to be used. Cut Dacron batting 1" smaller than board size. If the batting is not wide enough to cover the board in one piece, it can be seamed, but this is not advisable because the seam can separate or bulge, having an un-wanted effect on the print. If you must have a seam, do not overlap batting edges. Rather, place batting pieces edge to edge and use a long needle and sewing thread to whip-stitch edges together. If other paddings are used, cut them the same size as the print board. Cut covering plastic large enough to wrap around to the back of the board with about 3" overlapping onto the back.

Follow manufacturer's directions for applying with a roller, the linoleum or carpet adhesive to the cardboard and styrofoam surface. Attach corrugated cardboard to both sides of the styrofoam, one side at a time. *Pat* the cardboard down to make firm contact with the styrofoam. Do not use long strokes to smooth out the surface, because this will stretch the cardboard, eventually causing the print board to warp. Place the board on the floor, lay a piece of plywood over it and carefully walk on it to apply an even, overall pressure. Let dry according to manufacturer's directions.

Place Dacron batting over one side of the board. Using duct tape, tape the batting in place around the edges of the board, if necessary pulling the batting slightly to fit to the edge. There should be no wrinkles or bulges in the padding because, to print properly, the surface must be absolutely smooth. If other padding materials are used, pull tight and smooth, and tape in place around the edges of the board with duct tape.

With padding side down, center the board on the heavy plastic. Bring plastic around and over edges and to the back. Begin in the center of one side, taping plastic every 6″ with 6″-long strips of duct tape, pulling plastic out to the corner. Complete this side. Repeat on the opposite side, beginning in the center, pulling and taping plastic as tightly as possible while pulling out to corners. Tape corners last. Repeat the remaining two sides in the same manner. Plastic must be pulled taut with no waves or wrinkles. Clip excess plastic at corners. Place tape on corners to secure them. CAUTION: Plastic may loosen through use and will need to be restretched.

NOTE: A table or a stiff piece of plywood placed on a table can be converted to a print surface by covering them with padding and plastic. Follow the same procedure of pulling and taping described above.

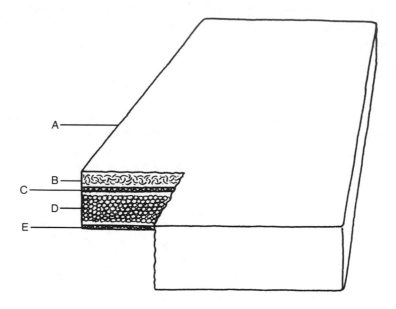

PRINT BOARD
(A) plastic covering (B) Dacron batting (C) and (E) corrugated cardboard (D) ¾″ thick styrofoam

Discussion

The usual objective in fabric printing is to obtain long lengths of a repeated pattern. Long print tables hold all the fabric needed for a particular run (or edition), so that the pattern on the screen can line up or register in a continuous repeat. The screen is moved down the length of the fabric. The fabric must remain in place while drying, so that any additional colors printed will also register.

In paper printing, the design does not have to be continuous. The screen can be stationary and is usually attached by two hinge-clamps to a table slightly larger than the print frame. One sheet of paper after another is registered under the screen. The screen is lowered, squeegeed, and the paper is removed for drying. Another screen for adding a new color is placed in the clamps, and the process is repeated for the desired number of prints.

By contrast, in polychromatic printing, all the colors of a print are printed at one time. There is no continuous, exact repeat, because the colors change in each print of the edition. The edition is limited to five to eight prints. Long print tables are unnecessary. All the fabric can be prepared for printing, and the small screens moved from panel to panel. Refer to diagram, page 71. As in paper printing, larger screens can be placed in two hinge-clamps that are screwed onto a table which is slightly larger than the print frame. Raise the hinge clamps to the level of the print surface with small blocks of wood. The hinged screen allows the prepared fabric on print boards to be printed by the same method as paper. Narrow strips of wood can be nailed into the table on two sides to wedge and register the print board and the screen. Refer to diagram, page 71.

The print table and print board must not flex and must be stable to provide good registration and a clear print image. The recommended combination of styrofoam and cardboard for print board accomplishes this. A low table (about 28″) permits a long reach on larger screens, so that maximum pressure can be exerted on the squeegee. Plywood or a table may also be padded and covered to make a print surface.

Padding must be used to ensure complete contact between fabric and screen. Fabric "gives," or stretches slightly, as the squeegee passes over. Also, the slight texture of the fabric prevents good contact without padding. Paper, on the other hand, is usually smooth and does not stretch, and is often printed on a hard surface.

The padding should be firm. If it is too spongy, it will cause the print to blur. Texture, folds, or unevenness in the pad will cause inconsistent screen contact. Dacron batting is suggested, because it is inexpensive, available in wide widths, and does not disintegrate. Industry uses thick felt.

The covering over the padding must not have texture. It is pulled tight over the print surface and must flex with the padding, but not slacken over time. A washable surface is convenient. Neoprene sheeting (a type of rubber), heavy gauge plastic, and oilcloth have the best required qualities. Neoprene is expensive, and it is best to have it professionally stretched on a table, but it can be pulled tight enough by hand and tacked or stapled with a heavy duty stapler. Refer to directions, page 19, for plastic and oilcloth covering. Another common pad covering is canvas. Its disadvantage, however, is that it is not washable. An absorbant backcloth, usually of muslin or a similar fabric, is pinned on the canvas. The fabric for printing is pinned onto the backcloth. Refer to page 68 for pinning directions. The backcloth will absorb excess dye, which can wash out later. When printing with lightweight fabrics such as scarves, the absorbent backcloth method is better than the plastic covered print surfaces. Heavy plastic makes a good covering for padding, because it is easily available, inexpensive, and washable. Another consideration in choosing a covering is ease of attaching the fabric for printing. Refer to "Stretching the Print Fabric," *Discussion*, page 68.

It is best to use the prepared print surface only for printing. An easily removable print surface will convert back into a work table. Styrofoam boards are also good for this reason.

5
Where to Print

The print process is affected by the weather. If the weather is damp, rainy or cold, or the work space is unheated or uninsulated, dyes, resist and prints will take longer to dry. In prolonged humidity, drying will be difficult, causing the resist to begin to dissolve, in which case the dyes will bleed together. A fan heater or hair dryer can be used to aid drying, but be careful not to hold it too close to the screen—the resist could become baked into the screen and be very difficult to remove, or the polyester screen mesh could melt.

In dry, cold weather or in hot weather, prints will dry very quickly—sometimes within minutes. They may be ready immediately after printing to be rolled in plastic for batching. Some fabrics can be sprayed with a fine mist of water to redampen them, although others will spot from the spray mist. Extreme weather conditions may also make the resist difficult to clean out of the screen, if it dries out too much. Try adding more Inko resist to help the white glue break down faster. Test a small area of the screen first.

Use proper lighting for accurate reflection of colors. Natural daylight or incandescent light shows colors more truly. Fluorescent lights tend to affect colors by casting a blue tint; however, full spectrum fluorescent lights are now available.

6

Work Space Arrangement
and Process Organization

Work space should be organized according to print processes. Mixing of the dyes and clearing of blocked screens should be done far away from the print fabric, cleaned or prepared screens, and work surfaces. For efficient processing, have two tables: one to be used for painting the dye on the screens and for printing; the other for measuring, cutting, stretching, and rolling the fabric in plastic. Keep powdered or liquid dyes and print paste away from the print fabric at all times. With this arrangement, two processes can be occurring simultaneously.

While the resist is drying on the screen and later, when the painted dye is drying, the print fabric can be cut and stretched, and the print paste can be prepared. While the prints are damp-drying for batching, the print screen can be cleaned, and the plastic sheets for batching can be cleaned and laid out ready to roll the prints. Also, the tape can be taken off the edges of the fabric. In doing this, be careful not to move the printed fabric, as dye may have seeped onto the plastic print surface.

7

Well Calculations
and Tracing Design on Screen

Summary

The objective is to size the design to stay within the print area of the screen and still allow enough room for wells to border the design.

The design can be drawn first on paper, then placed under the screen, and the lines traced onto the screen. The design will be marked on the screen with resist, a glue-like substance that blocks the screen. (Refer to "Resist," page 33.)

Sections to follow: Materials; Well Size; Tracing Design on Screen; and Discussion.

Materials

Tracing or drawing paper. Large enough to fit design size.

Pencil or felt-tip pen. For drawing design on paper.

Water-soluble pen or pencil. For marking the screen. Available at fabric or art supply stores.

Well Size

To determine the design's maximum size, the wells of the screen must be calculated. The wells hold the print paste away from the design between each pull. Along the screen's length (perpendicular to the pull of the squeegee), the wells must measure at least 1". The squeegee length must extend at least ½" into these wells on each side. The wells at the top and bottom sides of the screen should measure 2″-3″. The center area, bordered by the wells, is the largest printable area. The design must fit within this space. (Refer to diagram, page 15.) The size of the wells can always be increased to accommodate smaller designs.

Tracing Design on Screen

Mark on the drawing or tracing paper the available print area which fits the screen size being used. Within this area, use a pencil or felt-tip pen to draw the design in bold lines. The design will be traced on the screen and marked with resist. Resist blocks the screen where it is applied, preventing the print paste and dye from printing onto the fabric. This allows the fabric's original color to show, and therefore the line can be used as a design element. Another function of the resist is to hold the dye from bleeding and spreading when applied to the screen. This gives a distinct separation between colors, if the resist is applied in a design with enclosed shapes. (Refer to *Discussion*, page 30 for design considerations.)

Place the paper with the design drawn on it under the screen, frame side up, so the screen is contacting the paper. Lightly trace the design on the screen with washable pencil or pen. Be careful not to press too hard with the drawing implement, so that it does not damage or shift the screen mesh. Do not use a common lead pencil or ball-point pen, as they will not wash out of the screen, making it difficult to follow the outlines of future designs. If the design does not have to be marked in exactly, the marked paper can be placed under screen, frame side down. The resist can then be applied directly onto the screen by looking through the screen to the drawing outlines (but the design when printed will be reversed from the drawing if done in this manner).

A

B

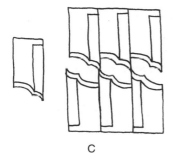

C

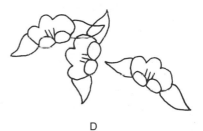

D

DESIGN FORMATS

(A) enclosed shapes (B) line drawing with no enclosed shapes (C) continuous repeated image (D) an isolated image printed many times

Discussion

Polychromatic printing combines both screen printing and hand painting on fabric. It results in a printed image that appears to look as if it is directly painted on the fabric or paper. In fact, the image is painted on the print screen and then transferred to paper or fabric with a pull of the squeegee. Many effects obtained from hand painting fabric and screen printing can be duplicated by polychromatic printing. However, the image can be only as large as the screen size, and the intensity of the colors in the image changes with each printing. These limitations can easily be used to advantage, as suggested in the following five ideas on format.

1. Often textile screen printing involves an image or motif that repeats along the length of the fabric. This image is usually lined up or registered with the previous printed image so that the pattern is continuous. The polychromatic process can do this as well. However, the polychromatic process produces fewer prints (five to eight per edition), and the colors of the prints change from dark to light, neither of which happens in traditional screen printing.

If a design in polychromatic printing is to be used in a continuous repeat, drawings can be made to check the design repeat sequence. Decide how many repeated images are needed, then cut that many sheets of tracing paper to the size of the screen's print area (this print area can be scaled down if it is too large to manage). On each sheet of tracing paper, draw or print the image that will be on the screen. If carbon paper is placed between each sheet and the image drawn firmly on the top sheet, the image will lighten through each layer in the same way it does in the printing process. These sheets can be arranged and lined up next to each other in the order in which they will be printed.

Remember, the sheets can be turned around to line up different sides of the design, but they cannot be turned over to reverse the image, because the screen cannot be turned over in printing.

2. Instead of a continuous repeated image, as in traditional textile screen printing, the repeats might be thought of as separate panels. The panels can be used individually or hung together, as illustrated by the wall hanging on the front cover of this book.

A reverse image can be obtained if printing is done in separate panels. The image must be printed on a fabric that allows the dyes to penetrate completely, so that the fabric is reversible. The thin- through medium-weight fabrics listed in "Fabric Categories," page 59, will usually give complete dye penetration.

3. Printing fabric for garments can be done on two or more screens, if one screen is not large enough. For instance, the sleeve and back of the garment can fit on one screen, and a sleeve and front on another screen. The outline shape of each garment piece can be marked in resist on the screen, and the design worked within this shape. If the screens are painted and printed in immediate succession, the coloration will be consistent throughout. The angle, pressure, and number of pulls of the squeegee must be identical on each screen to release the same amount of dye. Different fabrics can be printed within a print series, but the order must stay the same for all the screens. For example, the second print of each screen is printed on satin to give the same color intensity on each part of the satin garment.

4. An isolated image can be painted on the print screen (refer to diagram, page 29). To give the wells the outline of the image, cut the image out of newspaper. Use the newspaper to block the entire screen, except for the image area to be printed. If the image has a complicated shape, cut out the general shape, making sure the newspaper does not overlap into the paint image. Print paste with no dye in it can then be squeegeed across the screen to transfer the painted image. The edge of the cut newspaper shape will not show, because the print paste has no dye in it. If there are several isolated images painted in the print area of the screen, the wells can be masked in the usual manner (refer to "Masking Screen for Wells," page 50). Again, use clear print paste so that only the isolated painted shapes will show when printed.

5. The dyes are transparent, so one image superimposed over another can cause color changes and shadow effects. Refer to "Other Ideas for Polychromatic Printing," page 97.

Where the recommended resist is used, there will be a thin line exposing the print fabric. The tjanting tool can be worked much like a pencil or ink pen on paper. The line can be used as a design element, similar to a drawn line, becoming thicker or thinner to emphasize or subdue areas. Illusionary space can be created by drawing detailed or heavy lines in the foreground of an area and thin, sparse, or vague lines as the image recedes. Crosshatching, as is used in etching, can be drawn by making thin lines, first close together, then less dense, to emphasize shape and dimension.

The resist line is less obvious on fabrics in which the printed image bleeds slightly into the resist line area during the batching process. This happens on some thin fabrics. In some cases the resist line does not have to be used at all, and the dyes can be painted directly on the print screen and left to bleed. If a cotton organdy or silk organza screen is used, the painted dyes will not bleed at all, and the process and the result will be similar to painting on paper. Refer to Appendix C, page 106.

In polychromatic printing, colors in many areas of a design can be shaded, an advantage over regular screen printing. This can easily be done in small areas using a paintbrush and in large areas using an airbrush. Refer to "Dye Discussion," page 48. Shading adds dimension and the feeling of space to the flat fabric plane. Remember that dark colors tend to recede and light colors come forward. However, sometimes the size and placement of a color shade can also bring a color forward, or make it recede. Experiment and test the design by painting it on paper.

The section "Other Ideas for Polychromatic Printing," page 96, gives further suggestions on design elements and achieving special effects.

8
Resist

Summary

The objective is to apply an adequate amount of resist to the screen, preventing the dyes from bleeding and the print paste from passing through the screen.

The tjanting tool is used to apply the resist in a thin line. Use a paint brush for larger areas. The resist must dry thoroughly before dye can be applied to the screen.

It is not necessary in polychromatic printing to use resist. Dyes can be painted directly on the screen and left to bleed. Do not get painted dyes in wells, because the print paste will pick up dye and streak it across the print. To prevent this, use resist to mark wells (unnecessary with permanent masked wells).

Sections to follow: Materials; Recipe; Application; and Discussion.

Materials

Inkodye resist. Obtained through fabric print supply stores and through Inkodye screen process suppliers.

Wilhold or Sobo white glue. (Refer to "Where to Buy Materials" page 101.) NOTE: *Do not use* Elmer's or extra-strength new formula white glues. Some will curdle when mixed and/or will not wash easily out of screen. Try fabric white glues.

Mixing bowl.

Water.

Plastic squeeze bottle. For storing resist.

Tjanting tool. Large hole .05375" (inside spout diameter).

Paint brush. A firm, nylon bristle, flat-edge or pointed brush.

Paper towels.

Resist Recipe
One part Inkodye resist
One part Wilhold white glue or Sobo glue

Mix two ingredients thoroughly in mixing bowl. Add water slowly, until the mixture is of a consistency to run evenly through the tjanting tool. It should not flow too quickly (like water) or too slowly, which will result in a broken line. The consistency should be somewhere between that of heavy and light cream. Check the consistency by drawing on the screen. The resist will flow from the tjanting tool when the tip makes contact with the screen. The tool is gently dragged along the screen at a steady pace, like a pen. Store the resist in a capped squeeze bottle. If it becomes lumpy because the bottle was left uncapped, or because of improper mixing, pour it through a fine strainer to smooth the mixture.

Application
Place the screen flat on a table with the screen side up. This will reverse the direction of the design. Or, so the design is not reversed, place the frame side up with books at each corner to raise it off the table. The screen should not touch the table surface.

Cover the tip of the tjanting tool with a finger and fill the reservoir with resist. Refer to photograph, page 35. Tap the point of the tjanting tool against something hard to start the resist flow. Placing a finger over the tip will stop the resist flow. Hold the tjanting tool so that the *point* is at a 45 degree angle. This angle allows the resist to form a beaded line, filling the drawing line with the maximum amount of resist. (Refer to illustration, page 36.) If the resist line is thin or broken, it will not hold the dye in place. The resist may also be applied with a paint brush in large areas. Be sure to mark off wells around design area with resist (but not if using permanent wells), so that dye does not go into them. CAUTION: Avoid any large drops of resist that dry in raised lumps, preventing good screen contact when printing.

FILLING TJANTING RESERVOIR WITH RESIST

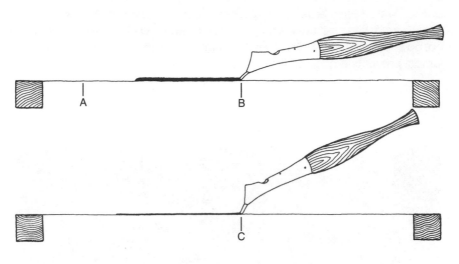

APPLICATION OF RESIST
(A) Cross section of the print screen showing the correct beaded line of resist
flowing from (B) the 45 degree angled point of the tjanting tool. (C) The tjanting
point is flat against the screen forming an inadequate resist line.

Let the resist air-dry for approximately half an hour or, for faster results, dry in the sun before painting dye onto the screen. Don't use extreme heat to help dry the resist, because this will bake it into the screen, making it difficult to remove later. Keep the screen horizontal at all times to prevent the resist from dripping or changing location.

To remove unwanted resist lines or drops before drying, rub the lines with wet paper towels, until no trace of resist is left in the screen. This should be done very carefully, so as not to smear or wash out any other resist lines. Once the resist is dry the only way to remove unwanted resist is to wash out all the resist and start again. (Refer to "Cleaning After Printing," page 85.)

Discussion

In polychromatic printing, dyes are applied to the screen and allowed to dry. The squeegeeing of print paste across the screen releases the dyes and transfers them to the fabric. The moment the dyes touch the screen, they bleed uncontrollably. To expand the artistic possibilities of the polychromatic technique, I found it was necessary to develop a method for curtailing this dye spread. In general, better control of materials allows a wider range of expression.

I approached this problem by thinking of the screen as fabric (which it is, of course) and considering the process by which dye is applied and controlled in fabric painting. Batik artists use hot wax flowing through a tjanting tool in a thin line. This line of wax penetrates the fabric completely. The wax is a resist and has two functions that are relevant to polychromatic printing.

First, resist ensures a definite separation of dye colors. Second, the resist prevents dye and print paste from bleeding or printing in unwanted areas. Thus, resist can be used as a design element. Refer to "Tracing Design on Screen," page 31.

The resist has a third function, one which is unique to polychromatic printing. It is important that the dye fully saturate the screen. The more dye in the screen, the more dye can be released for printing. The resist line holds dye, allowing a sufficient application.

Resist is not a necessity in poychromatic printing. It is only one way of controlling the dyes. The dyes will not bleed on a silk organza or cotton organdy screen (refer to Appendix C, page 106). Or, dyes can be left to bleed and create interesting effects. A word of caution: No dyes can be in well areas, because the print paste will absorb them and possibly streak dye across the print during squeegeeing. Marking the borders of the print area with resist will prevent the dye from spreading into them. With permanently masked well areas this precaution is unneccesary.

There are several considerations in deciding which resist to use on the print screen. The resist must last through the relatively short polychromatic printing process. Conventional agents for blocking the print screen can be used in polychromatic printing in place of other suggested resist methods. However, in traditional screen printing, the number of prints is far more than the five to eight prints obtained in the polychromatic process, so the conventional blocking agent holds up much longer than the resist suggested for polychromatic printing. The printing process will be easier if the resist washes out of the screen without much effort. If a tjanting tool is used, the resist must be able to be thinned or thickened to regulate the flow. Wilhold white glue and Inko resist meet the requirements; with experimentation, other products may be found satisfactory.

Blocking agents for traditional screen printing may be used in combination with the polychromatic method. Blocking agents are generally solvent-soluble or water-soluble. One principle in selecting a blocking agent is that if the ink or dye is water-soluble, the agent used is water-insoluble. The reverse applies for solvent-based inks or dyes.

In polychromatic printing, this principle does not have to be followed, as demonstrated by the suggested water-based resist of Wilhold glue and Inko resist, which lasts through all five to eight prints, then breaks down with water to wash out of the screen. Unfortunately, traditional water-based blocking agents usually do not hold up long enough when water-based dyes and print paste are used. Most blocking agents that clean with solvents work better, but the solvent residue must be thoroughly removed. Clean the screen with detergent and water and rinse out all the detergent. Any residue on the screen may affect the dyes.

Blocking agents can be further divided into four main groups: hand-cut stencils, directly applied block-outs, resist stencils, and photo stencils and photo emulsions. Each group includes solvent-soluble and water-soluble materials. The exceptions are photo emulsions, which are usually removed with bleaches, and photo stencils, which are removed with enzyme cleaners. These photo techniques may be used with either solvent-based or water-based inks or dyes.

Hand-cut stencils are often lacquer-based or water soluble films. The films are purchased with a clear plastic or paper backing. Plastic backing is superior, because it is stiff and easily peels away from the film. Films come in many colors and choosing one is a matter of preference. The negative areas of the design are carefully cut out of the film layer with a very sharp stencil knife. The backing must not be cut, because it is used to hold the positive shapes of the design in place. The screen is placed on top of the cut film and either solvent or water is rubbed through the screen to melt the film slightly, adhering it to the screen. Let the film dry before gently peeling off the backing sheet.

Directly painting, drawing, or otherwise applying a blocking agent to the screen can be a fast way to obtain a printable image. Water-soluble agents include block-outs (also called fillers or stencil fillers), glues, and tusches. Water-resistant materials include soft waxy crayons, litho pencils, tooshes, glues, lacquers, varnishes, and block-outs. Remember that the areas blocked on the screen keep the ink or dye from printing and are often the negative parts of the design.

If a positive image is wanted from a direct screen painting or drawing, use a resist stencil. Apply a water-soluble blocking agent to the screen. Then coat the screen with a solvent-based blocking agent and let dry. The solvent-based blocking agent will not penetrate or will be resisted where the water-soluble image is present, and therefore can be washed out of the screen in those areas. Use water-based inks and dyes. Reverse the order for applying blocking agents to obtain a water-based blocked screen for solvent inks or dyes.

The blocking agents used in direct and resist stencils must last for the duration of the printing session and flex with the screen without cracking or chipping.

Photo stencils and emulsions are light-sensitive. The sensitized emulsions are squeegeed in a thick coat onto the screen. The stencils are a thin film on a plastic backing (similar to cut stencil film), which can either be purchased already sensitized or can be coated with a sensitizing agent at the time stencils are to be exposed. A positive image, usually in opaque black on a clear plastic (acetate, mylar, or vinyl), keeps the light (sun, photo flood, or tungsten) from hardening the sensitized stencil or emulsion. A positive image can be derived from a photographic negative by changing it to a halftone positive (a service offered by some photographic stores.) A positive image can also be obtained by painting or drawing on clear acetate with engrossing black (similar to India ink), red acrylic paints, photo-opaque, or rub-on or dry transfer graphic aids.

Immediately after exposing, wash out the entire emulsion-coated screen or stencil with water. The soft, unexposed areas will dissolve. To adhere the stencil, press it onto the screen immediately after washing out the positive image. When it is dry, gently peel off the backing sheet.

Photo stencils and emulsions can give a high degree of detail quickly, compared to other screen-blocking methods. The positive image on plastic can be stored and re-exposed many times in order to save the art work. This is an advantage over methods in which the screen must be saved in order to save the image.

Remember, a highly detailed image requires a fine mesh screen for high resolution.

9

Dye Procedures

Summary

The objective is to apply the dye to the screen, without blocking it, in a sufficient concentration for printing the full edition.

The dyes are painted on the print screen within marked resist lines. The dyes may be painted outside the resist lines or with no resist to bleed together on the print screen. The dyes must be thoroughly dry before printing. Occasionally the dye concentration on the screen will be high and will block the screen holes when dry. The screen holes must then be unblocked before printing by clearing them with a stiff brush.

Sections to follow: Materials; Recipe; Application; Clearing Blocked Areas on Screen; and Discussion.

Materials

Fiber reactive dyes. Cibacron F dye is preferred, although Procion MX, Createx Cold Water Fiber Reactive Dyes will work also. Store powdered dyes in dark containers in a cool, dry area. Dye will lose its potency gradually, so check after storing two years.

Water.

Measuring spoons.

Small glass, plastic or stainless steel containers. Select small, tall jars to hold paint brushes without tipping. Aluminum and other metals should not be used, because they tend to react with dyes.

40

Paint brushes. Small, round, floppy Japanese bamboo or watercolor brushes are good for small areas and for detailing. Larger brushes may be used for larger areas.

Rubber gloves. A must at all times to protect hands from dye absorption.

Fine particle face mask. A must at all times when working with powdered dyes. NIOSH-approved masks are recommended in preference to the thin dust masks commonly available.

Small stiff brush. ½"-wide natural bristle or nylon flat brush of the type used for acrylic or oil painting. If a stiff brush can't be located, try trimming bristles shorter. NOTE: Don't use a toothbrush. Bristles are spread out and can't brush a concentrated area.

Newspaper.

Paper towels.

Dye Recipe
One-half teaspoon fiber reactive dye powder
One tablespoon water

Use gloves and mask at all times when handling powdered dyes. Only gloves must be used at all times when dyes are liquid. Mix one-half teaspoon dye powder and one tablespoon water in small jar. Mix as much dye as needed in these proportions. If dyes are kept in the liquid state for more than two days, they tend to thicken and will block the print screen. Createx liquid dyes and other purchased liquid dyes can be painted on the screen without being diluted.

Dye Application
With the screen in its horizontal position over the table, screen side up, paint dyes to saturate the screen mesh within the resist lines. Refer to photograph, page 42. Don't over-saturate, since this forms drops of dye under the screen, which then dry and block screen areas. On the other hand, using too little will cause the holes in the mesh to open quickly, and the dye concentration will be weak.

PAINTING DYE ON PRINT SCREEN

Dry the screen horizontally to prevent dye from running and bleeding. Do not use extreme heat to dry the screen, because it will bake resist into screen.

Printing may begin after the dyes dry, or the screen may be stored away from moisture for weeks. The only limitations are that dyes become less potent over time and with humidity, and the painted image can be damaged if water falls on it.

If small drops of unwanted dye are in an area to be painted later, the drops will dissolve invisibly into the painted dye. However, if there are drops in an area where no dye is wanted, let the screen dry. Then paint clear water over the dye drops, let the water absorb the dye for a minute, and blot with a clean paper towel. Repeat this procedure if the dye is still visible.

If dye spills or drops on an already painted dry area, it will show. There is no feasible way to remedy this, except perhaps to paint over the area again. However, this remedy can increase the dye potency and may block the screen mesh.

Dyes can be diluted to obtain lighter colors. However, a diluted dye will fade faster during the print sequence. Dyes can be painted onto the screen without using resist lines, or can be painted outside of resist lines. Under these circumstances, the dye will tend to spread, lose its potency, and fade faster through the print sequence. Loss of dye potency can be overcome by painting the dye on the screen once, letting it dry, then painting an additional layer of dye over already painted areas. Usually, colors will mix if painted on top of each other. Dyes painted over already dry dye will leave a harder edge. Two notes of caution: (1) dyes painted over dyes result in a build-up on the screen and have a tendency to block the mesh; (2) at the very least, the entire outside edge of a printable area must be outlined with resist or be permanently masked, so that the dyes will not bleed into the wells. This prevents dyes in the wells from being picked up by the print paste and streaked across the print.

Refer to "Color Mixing," page 114, which explains other useful color principles for painting with dyes.

Clearing Blocked Areas on Screen
It is very important that the screen clearing be done *away* from the print area and *away* from fabric. This can be done outdoors if it is not windy or damp. Wear a fine dust mask to prevent breathing the dye dust.

Hold the screen up to the light and note where the dye has dried, blocking the screen mesh. Refer to photograph, page 44. If the dye is not yet dry, it

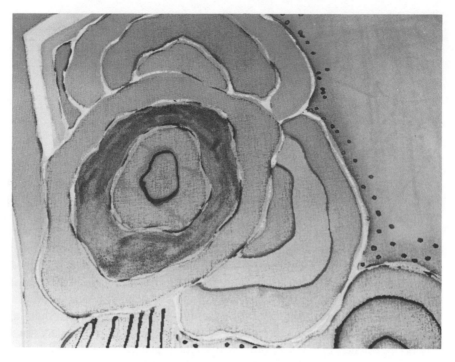

THE DARKER THIRD CIRCLE OF THE ROUND FLOWER
SHOWS DYE BLOCKING THE SCREEN MESH

can also appear as if the mesh is blocked. Lay the screen on newspaper in a horizontal position with the screen fabric face up and the frame side down. With a stiff, small brush, brush *only* the dye-blocked areas, one color at a time. Brushing clear areas will create unnecessary dye dust. The dye dust will fall onto the newspaper. Do not move the screen abruptly, because this will cause the dust to scatter. To see if blocked areas are clear, move the screen very slowly up to the light. When finished, roll up the newspaper slowly and throw it away.

It is, of course, best not to have to clear the screen. In most cases, it will be unnecessary to do this if the dyes are used immediately after mixing with water, mixed in the correct proportions, and not applied too heavily onto the screen.

Discussion

Dyes and Inks

The textile printer may choose either dyes or inks for color. Sometimes inks are referred to as pigments, but pigments are actually the coloring substance in inks. Inks can be purchased as separate components—pigment, binder, and extender—and mixed, or they may be purchased ready to use. Extenders are added to extend, lighten, and increase transparency while retaining the ink's consistency. Binders, or fixers, are added to bind the inks in a tough film around individual fibers. Textile inks are either water-based or solvent-based. Generally, paper printers use solvent-based inks because water will cause many papers to buckle. Dekaprint, Inko-Tex, Versatex, Euro-tex, and Createx fabric colors are water-base inks. Textile paints is another name for inks.

Inks tend to be opaque color mediums, although transparent inks are also available. (Dyes are transparent.) A lighter opaque color is obtained by mixing white pigment with a color. The bright white of fabric or paper showing through diluted colors will lighten transparent inks.

Usually a one-step application of heat fixes inks into the fabric. Dyes usually require two steps: introducing chemicals and applying heat and/or moisture.

Inks coat the fiber, which alters the feel (or hand) of a fabric, making it seem stiff. Lightweight fabric stiffens more than heavy fabrics. Washing may help soften the fabric. Inks also alter the fabric sheen and surface appearance. Dyes do not generally change the feel or surface sheen of the fabric, because they merge with the fiber molecules. Because inks coat the fiber, they can be used to print a wide range of synthetic or natural-fiber fabrics. They are unlike dyes in this respect, since dyes must be compatible with the fabric on which they are used, limiting the range of fabrics for each dye class.

One of the first considerations is selecting the correct dye class for the fabric to be used. Dyes for protein fibers (wool, animal hairs, etc.) use an acid for fixing. Cellulose fibers (cotton, linen, etc.) require alkaline fixatives. Although silk is considered a protein fiber, it is unique in that it can often be used with either acid or alkaline fixing dyes.

Acid dyes are commonly used for protein fibers. Dyes in this class use an acid for fixing. Acetic acid, the same acid found in lemons and vinegar, is often recommended as a fixative.

Kiton is an acid dye manufactured by Ciba Geigy chemical company.

Vat dyes for cellulose fibers were developed using the same principles as indigo vat dyeing. In indigo vat dyeing, dyes were fermented and steeped for days in large tubs or vats. Vat dyes are soluble. They are applied to the fabric and then, through an oxidation process, they turn insoluble, often change color, and become fixed. Ciba Vat Dye is one brand available to the artist. Inko dyes are a special vat dye that develops in sunlight instead of with oxygen.

Disperse dyes are used on 50-to-100 percent synthetic fabrics. Iron-on or heat-transfer dyes are usually in this class. This category of dyes can be painted or printed on paper, dried, and then iron-transferred onto the fabric. Disperse dyes are easiest to use as transfer dyes, but they are also available for bath dyeing. Deka Iron-on Transfer Paints, and Disperse Dye (distributed by Spectrum) are two brands of disperse dyes.

Union, or household dyes, such as Rit, Cushing, Tintex, Deka "Series L," and Color Easy dyes can be easily purchased at grocery, art and craft, variety, or fabric stores. These are all-purpose dyes made by mixing several classes of dyes in order to dye a wide range of fabrics the same shade. However, dye from the same package will produce different shades when, for example, a cotton fabric is dyed in the same bath with nylon, because some fabrics are more receptive and use up dye faster than other fabrics. Usually union dyes are an inefficient dye compared to dyes designed to react with particular fibers.

One of the newest classes of dye is fiber reactive dyes. These dyes are unique because some types of fiber reactive dye fix into fabric at lower temperatures than other dye classes. Reactive dye reacts with the fiber's molecular structure to form a strong chemical bond. These dyes are extremely colorfast and resistant to light.

Within this class are dyes that react with cellulose fibers, using salt or urea to assist the dye onto the fabric, and soda ash, baking soda, or TSP as an alkaline fixative. Other dyes react to protein fibers, using acetic acid or vinegar as a fixative. A few fiber reactive dyes fix on either cellulose or protein fibers, depending on whether an alkaline or acid fixative is used.

In addition to an alkaline or acetic fixative, heat and/or moisture are needed to fix the dye. Steam or the hot water in a dye bath supply heat and moisture when both are needed for a dye. Some dyes are more highly reactive and require only the moisture from a cold dye bath or batching to fix. A few dyes are so highly reactive that fixation can take place at room temperature over a period of hours. Unlike other dyes, the washing out of excess dye is a very important step in fiber reactive dyeing.

Fiber reactive dyes come in either liquid or powdered form. Liquid is often more expensive, but easier and safer to use. Health precautions must always be taken when using inks and dyes. Liquid or powdered dyes must be handled with gloves to prevent dyestuffs from entering the body. Lung irritations and allergies can be caused by inhaling dye powder. Wearing a NIOSH-approved fine-particle face mask is always a requirement when working with powdered dyes.

The average shelf life of most fiber-reactive dyes is two years. This means the color potency of reactives decreases gradually over time. Test old dyes to determine their color strength.

The best method for checking the colorfastness of dyes or any color medium is to put a sample of dyed or painted fabric or paper in a sunny window. (Be sure to save a control sample against which to measure changes). Check the color a week later. How does it compare with the control sample? This test is equivalent to approximately twenty years of average room light.

Another method for checking a dye's colorfastness and washability, is to run a dyed fabric sample through three or four washing machine cycles. (Again, save a dyed swatch against which to check.)

Createx Liquid Fiber Reactive Dye, Procion "MX" series (manufactured by the ICI chemical company), and Cibacron F (manufactured by Ciba Geigy chemical company) are fiber reactive dyes that fix at low temperatures and work on cellulose fibers. These dyes are recommended for polychromatic printing. Cibacron F will also dye protein fibers if vinegar is added. Cibacron F and Procion are powdered dyes. Sometimes the distributor changes the manufacturer's name. Cerulean Blue, Ltd. distributes Cibacron F under the name Fibracron Dye.

Choosing Dyes for Polychromatic Printing
Cibacron F is recommended for polychromatic printing. This dyestuff fixes easily with batching and requires very little washing out. Very little color change occurs between the mixed dye color and the finished color on the fabric.

Experimenting with different types and classes of dyes can open the polychromatic process to further versatility. However, there are several considerations when choosing a dye. In polychromatic printing, dyes are applied to a print screen, dried, and then must release easily when print paste or a similar substance is squeegeed through the screen. Therefore, the dye used must not permanently attach to the screen fibers, or it will not release onto the printing fabric. Consequently, most inks will not work well for polychromatic printing, because when they dry, they do not readily become soluble again.

In addition, it is best that the dyes painted on the screen do not block the screen mesh once they dry. Unblocking the mesh can release dye powder into the air. The powder can then settle on the screen or print fabric. Care in adjusting the concentration of dye can reduce this problem. Water is recommended for dissolving and adjusting the dye concentration. Some liquid dyes are dissolved in substances other than water. These dyes may block the screen mesh, react with other materials, or not dry on the screen. Sometimes adding a small amount of water will help.

Another consideration in dye selection is that the dye has a feasible method of fixing. The recommended reactive dyes use urea, an alkaline fixative (soda ash), and batching to fix the dyes. The chemicals and batching time can be altered, if necessary, to accommodate other types of cellulose fiber reactive dyes. For instance, Createx fiber reactive dye can be used if the urea is doubled and the batching time is extended to forty-eight hours. Sometimes increasing the urea will be enough to accommodate some dyes.

Dye Applications

The directions, page 41, explain how to use a brush to paint the dye on the screen to obtain an even color and maximum dye color strength. Dyes can also be watered down, applied unevenly, or left to bleed without restricting resist lines. Remember that less concentrated dye will lighten more quickly through the print series. This means that not so many print copies can be obtained.

In polychromatic printing, unlike other screen-printing processes, colors can be shaded wherever desired. This is accomplished through watercolor painting technique. Use larger brushes for large areas and work quickly so water and dyes do not dry before the area is completely painted. Enough clear water should first be painted on the screen to fill the mesh, but not enough to puddle. Paint only where the shading begins and not in any areas where full-strength color is desired. The water should extend to the resist lines or far beyond where the shading stops, because the dye does bleed and spread.

Apply the dye along the edge of the water and quickly fill in where full-strength color is wanted. Dip the brush in water to remove some of the dye. Then begin brushing the dye out into the water area with broad strokes. Work the dye so there is a gradual change from deep color to the white of the screen. Sometimes the full-strength area will need replenishing as the dyes bleed into the water. Instead of water, another color of dye can be used so that one color shades into another.

Shaded areas can be created using an airbrush. The same dyes used for printing can be used in the airbrush. Where shading is not desired, the screen should be covered with paper and edges of the area completely sealed with tape.

To shade an area with the airbrush, adjust the point and the spray button so a fine mist of dye is released. Move the point steadily and evenly across the screen, about twelve inches away from the surface (for small areas, move the airbrush closer). Build up the dye concentration by repeated dye applications, letting the screen dry between each spraying. The sprayed dye must never bead or saturate the screen mesh because it will then print unevenly. It is usually difficult to tell how much dye is on the screen. Experience will help you determine the proper amount. It is easier to shade small areas with a paint brush and use an airbrush for larger shapes.

10
Masking the Screen for Wells

Summary

The objective is to mask a border on the print screen, providing a place for the squeegee and print paste to rest away from print area and in between pulls.

For permanent wells, the screen is sealed with a masking compound. For temporary wells, paper strips, which mask the border, are taped in a few places on the screen, and when the print paste is squeegeed, the strips suction onto the screen.

Sections to follow: Materials; Directions for Print Wells; Permanent Masked Wells.

Materials

FOR TEMPORARY MASKING

Newspaper, roll of heavy paper, or brown paper tape. Papers or tape must be strong enough to keep print paste from seeping through. Newsprint is the thinnest that can be used.

FOR PERMANENT MASKING

Masking compound or Proseal. Sold in two components.
Throw-away rubber gloves.
Throw-away plastic mixing bowl and stirring stick.
Throw-away paint brush. Inexpensive, 1" wide, stiff.

Newspaper or large piece of paper. For covering screen.
Masking tape.
Measuring tape.

Directions for Temporary Wells

The size of the wells will have been previously determined. (Refer to "Well Calculations and Tracing Design on Screen," page 27.) The screen must be placed frame side down, so the screen fabric is above the table surface. To use paper as a temporary mask for the wells, cut four paper strips to fit from the resist-marked edge of the design to the outside wooden edge of the frame, along the length of each side. Using masking tape, tape the strips of paper in place in a few spots. Once the print paste has been squeegeed on, its suction will hold the paper onto the screen. Trim any flaps of paper hanging over the frame, so they do not get in the way of printing.

To use masking tape or paper tape for a temporary well mask, the strips should be lined up so they slightly overlap along the length of the well, and so they cover the area between the frame edge and the marked resist line of the printable area.

In placing temporary masks, it is important that the frame be covered with paper or taped to the outermost edge. If this is not done, the print paste will seep under the frame and onto the print fabric.

Permanent Masked Wells

Permanent wells on permanent screens require masking—a tedious process. (Refer to "Permanent Frame," page 13.) Screen print supply outlets do offer the service of masking wells with compound. This is expensive, so you may want to do it yourself, in which case, here is the method to use.

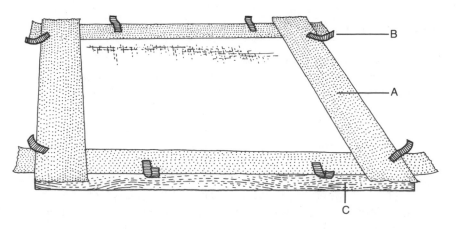

TEMPORARY WELLS

(A) Paper strips are held in place by (B) masking tape on (C) the back of the print screen, frame side down, so that the screen fabric is above the table surface.

Work in a well-ventilated room or outdoors, because fumes from the permanent masking compound are dangerous. Determine largest print area possible on the screen and use the largest possible squeegee. (Refer to "Well Calculations and Tracing Design on Screen," page 27.) Mark the largest print area clearly, using a ball-point pen and straight edge. NOTE: Temporary paper masking strips can be used in addition to the permanent mask when printing smaller areas. Cover the print area on both sides of the screen completely with paper and seal with masking tape up to the pen line on all four edges. Make sure the printing area of the screen is well sealed with the tape, because masking compound is very difficult to remove. Have everything ready, because masking compound dries very quickly, once mixed. As an alternative, mix small amounts of the compound at a time. Follow the manufacturer's proportions for mixing the compound. Measure accurately to be sure compound will dry. Use throw-away gloves, disposable mixing bowl and stirring stick. Apply the compound with throw-away paint brush in well areas and along crack where fabric meets wooden frame. Form a good seal, so print paste will be unable to seep under frame edge. Paint both inside and outside of screen mesh.

Let compound dry thoroughly before using the screen. If the compound is tacky, try exposing it to the sun to aid in drying.

11
Print Paste

Summary
The objective is to mix the print paste to the correct consistency, so that it can be controlled for squeegeeing, and can pass through the screen to make a clean print.

The print paste has two functions. First, when pulled across the screen it acts as a wetting medium, releasing dyes onto the fabric for a print. Secondly, it carries the chemicals, urea and soda ash, used for fixing dyes in the fabric. To mix the print paste, add sodium alginate to "chemical water". Let it sit for a period of time for the alginate to dissolve. More chemical water can be added to obtain the correct consistency.

Sections to follow: Materials; Recipe; and Discussion.

Materials
Soda ash—must be 100 percent pure soda ash. NOTE: Washing soda does contain soda ash, but often has additives that react with dyes.

Urea.

Water.

Sodium alginate—a thickener. Low-viscosity, high-solids preferred. This mixes quickly and gives a smooth texture. High-viscosity, low-solids sodium alginate takes longer to mix and has a heavier texture, but it works for this process, is less expensive and smaller quantities are needed.

Two-quart plastic pitcher.

Blender. Optional but easier for mixing print paste.

Large plastic or stainless steel mixing spoon.

Measuring cups.

Recipe for Chemical Water for Cibacron F
2 tablespoons soda ash
2 tablespoons urea
4 cups tap water

Mix the above ingredients in a blender to dissolve chemicals. It is important to do this quickly to prevent the soda ash from hardening and becoming difficult to break down. If a blender is not used, mix the ingredients in a two-quart pitcher with a plastic or stainless steel spoon until the chemicals dissolve. Chemical water will last indefinitely if kept in the refrigerator. If other fiber reactive dyes are used, double the urea.

Recipe for Print Paste
4 cups chemical water
4-5 tablespoons sodium alginate, low-viscosity, high-solids, OR 2-3 table-
* spoons sodium alginate, high-viscosity, low-solids*

Put four cups of chemical water in a blender and blend at low speed. Slowly add the sodium alginate. Continue blending until it thickens and the surface no longer blends in (about two minutes). Immediately pour the print paste into a two-quart covered storage pitcher or jar. Most print paste can be stored in the refrigerator for up to three months.

To mix print paste without using a blender, sprinkle the sodium alginate *very slowly* into four cups chemical water in a two-quart plastic pitcher. Stir with a spoon very quickly. It may take two people, one to stir, one to sprinkle. NOTE: Print paste mixture has a tendency to lump if the sodium alginate is poured in too quickly. After mixing with a blender or by stirring, let the print paste sit 15 minutes if low-viscosity sodium alginate was used, or overnight if high-viscosity sodium alginate was used.

When ready to use the print paste, check its consistency. Do this using a large spoon to scoop up the print paste and let it fall from the spoon. If the stream breaks, it is too thick. To thin it, *slowly* stir in small amounts of chemical water. Do not use the blender again, because the mixture will be too thick. Check again with the spoon. The perfect print paste consistency is at the point at which the stream stops pouring and breaking and begins to flow in a steady ribbon. Be careful not to make the print paste too liquid. It should be slightly thicker than honey, and there should be no lumps.

An option is to mix both types of print paste in equal proportions to make a good consistency for printing. Do not mix the sodium alginate powders together. Mix them separately in the chemical water. Once the powders are dissolved, stir the print paste together.

Approximately ½ teaspoon of dye powder dissolved in a tablespoon of water per 4 cups of print paste can be added to the print paste to give a background color for the print. It must be a light-to-medium color. The print paste will appear very dark so check color by smearing a thin layer on white paper. If the color is dark, it will darken the other colors painted on the screen, so they will not show up in the print. When the dye is added to the print paste, the chemicals begin to react immediately, and a slow deterioration begins after 45 minutes. Because of this time limit, add the dye to the print paste just before printing begins.

Discussion

Thickeners

Print paste, which is usually composed of water and a thickening agent such as sodium alginate, is used to carry the dye (and sometimes the fixing agents) across the print screen. The thickening agent keeps dyes from bleeding on the fabric after it has been printed. The consistency must be correct—not so thin that it uncontrollably floods the screen, not so thick that it clogs the screen mesh or does not give a clear print. Ink printing does not require dye thickeners because inks are usually purchased in ready-to-use thickened form, or binders or extenders are added to ink pigment to obtain the correct consistency.

In polychromatic printing, the print paste has a unique function. When pulled across the screen, the print paste acts as a wetting medium, releasing the dyes that have been painted on the screen and allowed to dry, thus transferring them to the fabric.

Sodium alginate is made from a seaweed base and is harmless. In water.it immediately expands and dissolves to "thicken" the water. Some sodium alginate compositions react faster than others. There are many sodium alginates offering a variety of consistencies for a wide range of purposes. The resistance of a liquid to flow is called viscosity. The amount of sodium alginate needed to bring the liquid to the correct viscosity depends on its solids content. Low-viscosity alginates have characteristically high solids contents and require a higher ratio of powder to water than high-viscosity alginates. Observe how the thickener behaves when it flows off a dowel-like stirring rod. If it forms a steady stream, like heavy syrup, it has a "long flow." If it globs and sticks like loose gelatin, it has a "short flow."

The sodium alginate suggested for polychromatic printing has a high solid content, low viscosity, and a long flow. It is a lightweight syrupy substance, compared to the low-solid, high-viscosity thickeners, which are heavy, like taffy. The preferred sodium alginates are usually more expensive and larger quantities are needed to mix to the correct consistency. The advantages are that they dissolve faster and can be prepared in a shorter time. Other types of sodium alginate can also be used with good results.

The fixing agents (such as urea and soda ash) can be added to the print paste. This eliminates the extra steps of adding them to the fabric before printing, (letting the fabric soak in the agents and then dry) or of printing the dyes on the fabric, letting it dry, then painting it or immersing it in a bath of fixing agents. The latter is not very common, but dyes that fix this way must set very quickly, because the application of the fixing agent could cause them to bleed. The fixing agent must be evenly dispersed in print paste or evenly applied for uniform dye fixing.

Some fixing agents break down the sodium alginate. Disperse dyes work better using monagum thickener. The acid for acid dyes often curdles the sodium alginate. An acid donor can be used instead. It delays the release of acid until the print is steam-fixed. Thus, the acid does not affect the sodium alginate during the critical period.

The print paste in polychromatic printing should be thin enough so that an adequate amount can be squeezed through the screen to make a perfect print. If the print paste is too thick, the painted dyes on the screen will not release onto the fabric. If it is too thin, too much dye will release from the screen, and the print paste will be less controllable.

Fixing Agents
The recommended fiber reactive dyes (refer to page 104 for dye list) use urea in printing and painting on fabric and salt in bath dyeing. The urea and salt help the dye penetrate the fabric. Soda ash, baking soda (bicarbonate of soda), or TSP (trisodium phosphate) fix the dye onto the fibers. Soda ash is generally used for best results in batching and dye bath, and baking soda is used for steam settings. TSP is used for certain processes with Createx fiber reactive dyes.

12

Fabric Sequence for Printing
And Fabric Characteristics

Sections to follow: Guidelines for Fabric Sequence; Fabric Categories; Chart for Fabric Sequence; and Discussion.

Guidelines for Fabric Sequence

To achieve the maximum number of prints and give the best print results, you must choose the type of fabric which corresponds to the print sequence. The sequence of prints moves from dark and bright to lighter and less intense colors. Dye colors will be more vivid on white fabrics and duller on ecru, off-white, or pastel fabrics. Slick fabrics must be used for the first print to allow the maximum amount of dye to be released from a dry screen. Thin or medium weight fabrics are best for printing. Textured fabrics can be used only for the final print with a large screen, or for each print after the first with a small screen, because textured fabrics require a maximum amount of squeegee pressure to make good contact between the screen and fabric. While this is easy with small squeegees, it requires several pulls of a large squeegee which will exhaust the dye on the screen. Absorbent fabrics should be used on final prints because, if left in contact with the screen for 5 to 10 minutes, they act to draw the dye out of the screen. The recommended fabric sequence for the most satisfactory print results is outlined in the chart which follows on page 61.

Fabric Categories

Fabrics without finishes are best for printing. They must be natural fabrics such as 100 percent cotton, silk, viscose rayon, linen or a fabric with a

59

combination of any of these natural fibers. Test a small swatch of a fabric with a finish by printing a sample. In some instances, the dye may be able to penetrate the fabric fibers during the 24-hour batching period.

Some cotton fabrics, although untextured, may have a fine layer of fuzz that prevents large screens from making satisfactory contact with the fabric surface.

Shiny, Slick, Thin Fabrics
silk satin
silk charmeuse
silk nan shan pongee
silk shantung pongee
heavy China silk (12mm* or heavier)
silk taffeta

Medium Weight Fabrics
spun silks
Shen's pongee
Thai silk
silk broadcloth
heavier pongees
lawn cotton
cotton poplin
viscose rayon satin

Heavyweight and Slightly Textured or Fuzzy Fabrics
silk noil
cotton broadcloth
cotton sateen
cotton canvas
cotton muslin
viscose rayon challis
linen

Highly Absorbent Fabrics
silk satin
silk charmeuse
silk broadcloth
raw silk
viscose rayon challis
viscose rayon satin

**Unsatisfactory Fabrics for
   Printing**
*pile fabrics (velvets, corduroy)
highly textured fabrics (boucle,
   fabric from slubbed yarns)
lightweight fabrics (organdy, light
   China silks)
open-weave fabrics*

*"mm" is for momme, a unit of weight for silk—5mm is very light and 18mm is very heavy.
Pounds are also used, based on a 50 yard bolt of fabric. "4 lb" is equivalent to 8mm and "7 lb"
to 12mm.*

Chart for Fabric Sequence

Fabrics for Small Screens	**Fabrics for Large Screens**
FIRST PRINT	
shiny, slick, thin fabrics	shiny, slick, thin fabrics
color: white, off-white, ecru, pastels	color: same
MIDDLE PRINTS	
(prints 2-5 on small screens, prints 2-3 on large screens)	
shiny, slick, thin fabrics	shiny, slick, thin fabrics
medium weight fabrics	medium weight fabrics
heavy weight fabrics	
highly absorbent fabrics	
color: white, off-white, ecru, pastels	color: same
LAST PRINTS	
(prints 6-7 on small screens, prints 4 on large screens)	
same as for Middle Prints	same as for Middle Prints
color: white	color: white
THE FINAL PRINT	
same as for Middle Prints	same as for Middle Prints
highly absorbent fabrics are best	heavy weight fabrics
	highly absorbent fabrics are best
color: white	color: white

Discussion

Synthetic and Natural Fibers

Before this century, fibers were derived entirely from natural protein or cellulose materials. With the development of petroleum processing, synthetic fibers appeared on the market. A silk shortage in 1938 stimulated the development of nylon fiber. Dyes that fix on protein fibers, which include silk, will often fix on nylon, whose chemical makeup and properties are similar.

Silk also inspired the production of rayon, the first synthetic fiber. Rayon is manufactured from regenerated cellulose (cotton, wood pulp, etc.) through a process that actually alters the natural fibers. Dyes that fix to cellulose will usually dye viscose rayon.

Synthetics start as chemical solutions, then are forced or extruded through small holes to form continuous strands called filaments. These filaments are put into a chemical bath or air chamber to solidify. This process imitates the way, in nature, liquid silk is extruded thorough glands in the silkworm's head.

For fine, lightweight synthetic fabric, filaments can be used in single strands called monofilaments or in many strands, or multifilaments. These can be twisted together for strength and for heavier fabrics. Filaments can be shortened to imitate natural fibers. Shortened synthetic filaments are called "staples."

The best quality silk comes from the long, continuous filaments unravelled from silkworm cocoons. The filament is broken into staples when the moth leaves the cocoon. Cotton has one of the shortest staples. Staple fibers of wool are longer and those of linen are longer yet. Usually, the longer staples within each of these fiber types produce better quality fabric. Adding twist to the fiber gives strength.

There are many terms describing the length and types of fiber and the processing of silk. Spun silk is made from broken cocoons. The continuous filaments reeled off the unbroken cocoons are used for satin, charmeuse, etc. Dupion or douppioni has fibers that are uneven in diameter (slubbed), caused by two cocoons joining together. This fiber is used in pongee, shantung, nan shan, and other silks. Noil silk comes from the inner part of the silk cocoon, which has short fibers. Tussah, or wild silk, comes from silk worms whose diet and environment are uncontrolled, producing course, uneven fibers. Tussah and noil silk are often the least expensive fabrics. They are inaccurately referred to as raw silk.

Actually, raw silk is any silk yarn or fabric in which the gum (or sericin) has not been removed. The gum occurs naturally on the silk strand in the cocoon. It is usually removed after the fabric has been woven. Degummed silk is softer and more lustrous, and will take dyes better.

Weaves

Fabric is made up of warp threads running parallel with the selvedge edge and weft threads crossing perpendicular to the warp. How these threads cross determines the weave.

The most common weave is plain or tabby, in which the threads alternately go over and under one another. The characteristics of the threads, such as tightness and direction of twist, diameter, flexibility, smooth or slubbed texture, and the spacing of the threads in the weave all contribute to the variety of fabrics. Often slight variations in thread character distinguish one fabric from another, even though they are the same weave. Notice the many fabrics listed under tabby weave on page 64.

A few of the fabrics mentioned in this book are not tabby woven. In silk or rayon "satin" weave, the threads skip over several other threads (referred to as "floats") in an even pattern. The floats and the soft twist of the yarn expose the shiny filaments. Silk charmeuse is a satin weave of slightly lighter weight that is less shiny and has a more adaptable drape than silk satin. Cotton sateen is a satin weave with smaller floats to provide strength to short cotton staples.

Chart of Plain or Tabby Weaves

NAME OF FABRIC	TRADITIONALLY OR COMMONLY MADE FROM THESE FIBERS	CHARACTERISTICS OF THREAD
batiste	cotton	even, fine, thin
lawn	cotton	
china silk	silk	
organdy or organza	silk, cotton	even, fine, thin, stiff
georgette	silk	
voile	cotton, silk	highly twisted, less stiff
chiffon	silk	
percale	cotton	medium weight, even
muslin	cotton	
challis	rayon, wool	
broadcloth	silk, cotton	
pongee	silk	
shantung	silk	
nan shan	silk	
taffeta	silk	
sailcloth	cotton	heavy, even
canvas	cotton	
silk noil (raw silk)	silk	
boucle	silk	heavy, uneven
tussah	silk	heavy, uneven weft, fine warp
velvet	silk	heavy, tabby weave, with extra looped thread, which is cut
velveteen	cotton	
corduroy	cotton	loop cut in ridges
terry cloth	cotton	loop uncut
poplin	cotton	thread thin in one direction, perpendicular thread heavy (rib weave)
pongee	silk	
grosgrain	silk	greater difference between weights of perpendicular threads
crepe	cotton or silk	oppositely twisted
crepe de chine	silk	threads woven together

Fabric Finishes

Fabrics without finishes are recommended for bath dyeing, or when dyes are used in printing or hand painting. Manufacturers use finishes to affect the performance, look, and feel of the fabric. One example is permanent press fabrics, where the finish serves to prevent the fabric from wrinkling. Finishes are often made to last through many cleanings, so washing in strong detergent may not remove all the finish. A few finishes may break down enough with prewashing to allow dye penetration. To prewash, follow the preshrinking procedure, this page. Prewashing is not usually required for the recommended fabrics.

Because they lie on the surface, inks will often fix on finished fabrics. But finishes frequently make it difficult for dyes to penetrate. One exception to this is the printing process where batching is the fixing method. In bath dyeing and painting on fabrics, the dyes are in a proper fixing environment for only a short time; but batching can go on for days, if necessary, to promote penetration of some fabric finishes.

Preshrinking

Most of the recommended fabrics have not been preshrunk. The fabric will shrink when the dyes are washed out and during damp ironing. If a specific final size is required, as for fabrics used in garments, it is advisable to preshrink the fabric. Cotton may be preshrunk in hot water, but silk and rayon require lower temperatures. Five minutes in a warm, mild soap bath is adequate. Rinse in cold water, removing all soap. Wring out all excess water, then roll in a towel or spin dry. Iron damp fabric until thoroughly dry.

Less expensive silks and cottons tend to shrink more. Synthetics usually shrink very little and preshrinking is generally unnecessary.

Fabrics without finishes are obviously preferable to those with finishes, but they are not usually available in fabric stores, because retailers appeal to consumers of finished goods. Refer to page 103 for sources of unfinished goods.

13
Stretching the Print Fabric

Summary
The objective is to stretch tightly the fabric used for printing over the print surface in order to make even contact with the screen to produce a clear print.

The fabric is pulled and taped onto the print surface.

Sections to follow: Materials; Directions; and Discussion.

Materials
Fabrics—cotton, silk, viscose rayon, and linen with no sizing or surface finishes. Finishes may resist dye penetration. Fabrics cannot have too much texture, because it will interfere with the print screen contact. Iron the fabric if wrinkled. Cut fabric or tear it to be at least 1″ larger than print area. One large piece of fabric can be stretched for several prints. (Refer to preshrinking and prewashing, page 65, if needed. See "Fabric Categories," page 59, for types of fabric.)

Masking tape. At least ¾″ wide.

Directions
Make sure the prepared print surface is clean, dry and free of any dye. Fabric will be stretched and held in place on the print surface with masking tape. The fabric should be positioned so the screen frame rests at least ½″ in from the edge of the print surface, and, if possible, so the frame will not overlap another print. (Refer to diagram, page 71.)

Tape the fabric in place in two steps. First, begin taping on a selvedge edge, if possible. Hold a length of tape taut with thumb and forefinger of each hand. With both middle fingers, stretch fabric edge slightly and put a piece of tape over ⅜″ of the fabric edge. Refer to diagram below. Run side of fingernail along the edge of the fabric to assure tape contact. Second, with the fabric on the print surface, position the fabric and then run side of fingernail along tape to attach fabric firmly to the plastic surface. Repeat these two steps along the side of the fabric. Continue, taping the two sides at right angles to the previously taped side. Finally, tape the opposite edge. All edges of the fabric must be taped in place so the fabric is stretched smoothly and tightly across the print surface, before beginning the printing process.

If the tape comes off, it may not be covering a full ⅜″ of the fabric edge, it may not be firmly pressed onto the print surface, or the print surface may be wet or not clean.

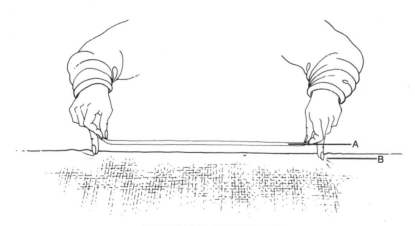

TAPING THE PRINT FABRIC
(A) Hold length of tape taut with thumb and forefinger of each hand. (B) With both middle fingers, stretch the print fabric edge slightly and place the tape over ⅜″ of the fabric edge.

Discussion

The fabric must stay in place under the screen as the squeegee passes over it. For the screen to make complete contact, the fabric must not buckle or wrinkle. Fabric can be held temporarily by a tacky surface, or it can be taped or pinned in place.

A light adhesive can be sprayed on a hard table or plastic-covered padded print surface to hold fabric in place. However, adhesive spray will stick only to a print surface that remains dry. Paper and T-shirt printers, whose inks or dyes do not penetrate through materials to the print surface, often employ this method.

Canvas-covered padded tables are usually made tacky by an application of wax. Thin the wax with mineral spirits until it is the consistency for spreading in a thin layer using a wide putty knife or squeegee. The fabric for printing can be rolled off tubes onto the wax surface. In a a fanning motion, one hand smooths and presses the fabric onto the wax, and the other hand pulls out the wrinkles. The tacky surface will last for many printings and can be washed off between printings with soapy water. To apply a new coat, first remove old wax by softening it with a warm iron and then scraping it off with a putty knife.

Straight pins or T-pins work well on a canvas surface, because the pin holes heal and disappear. At the edge of the fabric, the pin is initially inserted upright and pushed straight down through the padding. Then it is pushed at an angle toward the center, so that it holds more firmly. Work the same direction around the fabric edges as in taping. See page 67. Place the pins every four to six inches, stretching fabric taut.

Some people find taping faster than pinning. Tape works well on many surfaces, including plastic, oil cloth, and neoprene.

Both tape and pinning methods prohibit printing to the fabric edge. This may be a consideration in printing scarves with rolled or finished edges. When a design must reach the edge of the fabric, an adhesive or waxed print surface is recommended. For fabrics that stretch, such as crepes and knits, a tacky surface might also be advisable, since fabric can be held in place with overall contact.

14

Pulling Prints

Summary

The objective is to produce a clear print with one pull of the squeegee, releasing just enough dye and print paste onto the fabric beneath the screen.

Once the fabric is taped taut over the print surface and the masked print screen centered over the fabric, pour the print paste along top well. Place the squeegee behind the print paste. Pull the squeegee firmly across the screen at a 60 degree angle to force a thin coat of print paste through the mesh. This releases some of the dye painted on the screen into the fabric. The print paste is scooped onto the squeegee blade and returned to the top well. The screen is placed on the next piece of fabric, and the squeegee is pulled again.

Sections to follow: Material; Directions; and Discussion.

Materials

Waxed paper strips. For protecting a wet print if the frame must rest on it while other prints are being pulled.

Paper towels. For wiping the squeegee blade.

Large spoon. For scooping the print paste.

Large apron.

Rubber gloves.

READY TO USE FOR PRINTING:
   Dry, painted, unblocked, masked-out print screen.
   Squeegee. 1" wider than the design or print area.
   Stretched fabric. Check to make sure it has remained taut.
   Print paste in pouring pitcher. Add dye just before beginning to print.

NOTE: The help of another person may be useful in holding the screen if this is your first experience with printing, or if the screen is very large.

Directions
If the screen is cleared of blocked dye, there will be fine, invisible dust on it. In this case, the screen cannot be moved or slid over the fabric, or the dye dust will spread. Instead, it must be placed carefully and moved only when the print has been completely squeegeed. Place the screen squarely over the stretched fabric, avoiding the taped edges. The screen placement should allow a comfortable pull of the squeegee.

Have all materials ready and organized. Once the printing begins, there won't be time to locate them. Materials should include paper towels, waxed paper (if needed), print paste, large spoon, and squeegee. Decide on the print order of the fabrics, so you can move quickly to the next print area (see "Fabric Sequence," page 61). In the well at the top of the print screen, pour enough print paste evenly across the well to make at least one print. More print paste may be poured if the wells are large enough. It is very important not to let the print paste run into the print area. If this happens, the print paste will absorb the dye painted on the screen, leaving as pale spot on the prints pulled later.

If you feel the screen will slip, another person should hold the screen opposite you. Smaller screens can be held in place with one hand while squeegeeing with the other. Or, the front of the frame may rest against your body, so as you pull, the squeegee does not slide the frame forward, pulling the design out of place.

Wedge the squeegee against the frame so all the print paste is in front of the blade. With one hand at each end, hold the squeegee at a 60 degree angle.

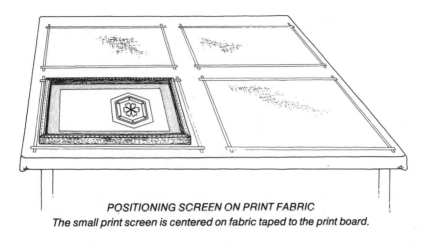

POSITIONING SCREEN ON PRINT FABRIC
The small print screen is centered on fabric taped to the print board.

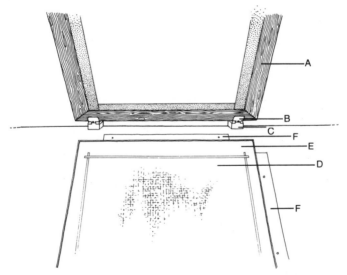

For (A) larger screens, place in (B) hinge clamps on (C) blocks screwed to work table. Lower screen onto (D) fabric taped on (E) print board. The board was registered under the screen by wedging against (F) two wood strips.

Apply as much downward pressure as you can at this angle, but not so much that it bends the blade down flat on the screen. Have the pressure evenly distributed across the squeegee. Take a few seconds to pull the squeegee across the screen with an even, steady pull. Do not stop until all of the print paste is in the opposite well. Stopping at any point across the print will leave a fine line across the fabric. (Refer to diagram below.)

When the pull is completed, scoop all the print paste onto the blade by tilting it back and pushing it against the frame edge. Lift the print paste and return it quickly to the back well. Rest the squeegee and print paste in the well. The print paste should be in *front* of the squeegee.

Lift one corner of the screen slightly to observe whether good print contact was made. If the contact was bad, the screen will still register when replaced on printed fabric. Squeegee across the screen again. To reach the full potential of polychromatic printing, it is best to squeegee correctly once per

PULLING PRINT

(A) Pull squeegee at a 60 degree angle to force a thin layer of (B) print paste through screen mesh. Return squeegee and print paste to the far well again and rest squeegee on (C) dowels or nails inserted at each end.

print, because the more times a print must be squeegeed, the more dye is released on that print, and the less is left for the remainder of the prints. Also, the longer the screen is left on the print, the more dye will be absorbed into the fabric. This may or may not be a design advantage.

When good print contact has been made, move to another area of the fabric by lifting the screen off the print. Holding it level, place it squarely over the next fabric area to be printed, again avoiding the tape. Repeat the same squeegeeing process. Continue printing in this manner until the dye on the screen is exhausted. On the last print, the screen can be squeegeed several times and left on the fabric for 5-15 minutes to let any remaining dye on the screen be absorbed into the fabric.

Discussion

One of the goals of polychromatic printing is to obtain as many prints as possible before the dyes are exhausted from the screen. Pulling the squeegee correctly is essential. The squeegee controls the amount of print paste forced through the screen. The print paste transports the dyes from the screen to the fabric.

Considerations for correct squeegeeing:

1. *The flexibility and shape of the blade edge.* Refer to "Print Screen Construction and Squeegee Size," page 17.

2. *The angle at which the blade is held while squeegeeing.* The suggested angle is 60 degrees, but this can vary slightly. In a more upright position, less print paste and dye are released. Care must be taken with the squeegee in the upright position that the bottom edge of the squeegee is free of print paste. If it is not, it can drag dots of print paste across the screen.

3. *The amount of pressure on the squeegee.* Maximum pressure is recommended, but not so much that the blade bends down flat on the screen. Full pressure is required for two reasons. First, this will release a smaller amount of print paste through the screen. Second, the pressure aids in good contact between the screen and fabric. Though only a small amount of print paste is released, the pressure will force that small amount to make contact with the fabric. Pressure must be evenly distributed across the blade and constantly applied through the entire pull of the print; otherwise, uneven printing will occur.

4. *The pace of the squeegee.* Pulling the squeegee very quickly across the screen using great pressure will release less print paste. This is excellent for lightweight fabrics, but some medium-to-heavy or slightly textured fabrics will not make good contact with the screen if squeegeeing is done too fast. For polychromatic printing, take a few seconds to pass over the screen with as much pressure as possible.

5. *The number of times the squeegee passes over the screen.* In polychromatic printing, the squeegee should be pulled over the screen only once, to release the least possible amount of dye. To obtain identical results with each print on a given type of fabric or paper, you must keep the factors mentioned above the same throughout the edition. Establish a rhythm of the same angle, pressure, and pace.

Two other important factors determine print quality: the padding of the print surface, and the consistency of the squeegeed substance (the print paste). Refer to discussions on print surfaces, page 23, and print paste, page 56, for further details.

T-shirt printing demonstrates how these factors are used in combination. T-shirts are usually printed on a narrow, unpadded board placed between the shirt's front and back layers. The knit is pressed into light adhesive on the board to hold it in place for printing. A medium-stiff, round-edged squeegee is used to leave an adequate deposit. A lot of pressure is applied to the squeegee to force the ink or print paste into the knit. Several passes of the squeegee may be necessary to achieve an adequate print.

15

Batching

Summary

The objective is to keep the printed fabric damp for 24 hours or longer to fix the dye in the fabric.

To batch the printed fabric, roll it in plastic to keep it damp. After 24 hours or longer, remove the printed fabric from the plastic and rinse it in cold water to remove any remaining print paste and excess dye. (Refer to "Washing Off," page 80.)

Sections to follow: Materials; Directions; and Discussion.

Materials

Large sheets of plastic. Clear if possible, so dye can be easily washed off, and plastic reused. Purchase enough plastic so the printed fabric can be placed on it without overlapping and still leave at least a 6″ heading at one end of the plastic sheet.

Fine-misting spray bottle. Used to dampen prints that dried too fast.

Rubber gloves.

Directions

Wait to begin batching until prints become damp and the print paste is absorbed into the fabric. This may occur immediately or as much as 20 minutes later. Remove the tape and lift the printed fabric straight up and off the printing surface, so any dye remaining on the plastic surface will not be

75

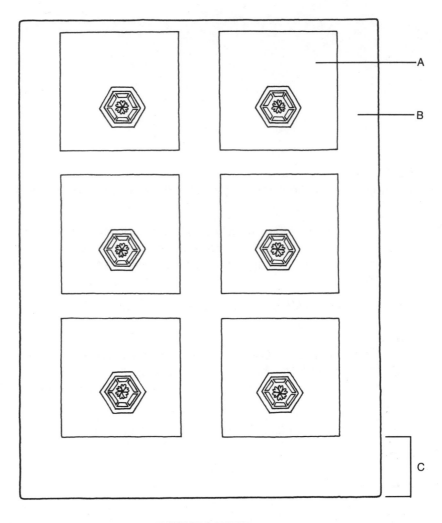

BATCHING PRINTS
(A) The damp printed fabric is placed on (B) plastic leaving at least a (C) 6" heading at one end.

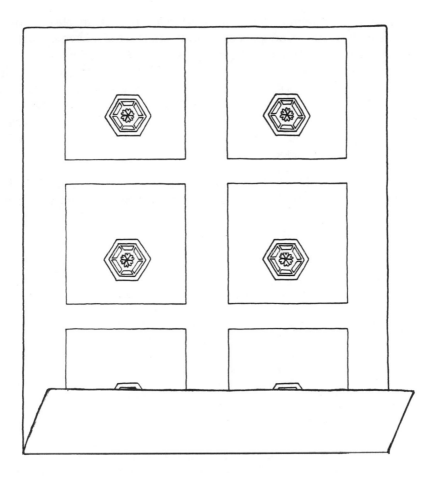

BATCHING PRINTS
The heading is folded over fabric and the rolling can begin towards the opposite side.

rubbed onto the fabric. Place printed fabric on a clean plastic sheet. Be sure prints do not overlap, or dye may be transferred. Leave at least a 6" heading of plastic. (Refer to diagram, page 76.) Fold this edge over the printed fabric. Continue rolling the printed fabric and plastic towards the other end. Check to see that there are no folds in the printed fabric. Folds will also cause the dye to transfer. The long roll of printed fabric should be folded and stored at room temperature for at least 24 hours for Cibacron F dyes or 48 hours for other dyes. Do not store longer than seven days, because the fabric may begin to mildew.

If the printed fabric dries before it is rolled in plastic, it can be redampened by misting with a spray bottle. CAUTION: On some fabrics, the mist will leave spots.

Discussion

Most dyes need heat, moisture, and one or more fixing agents to become fixed on the fibers. Sometimes, if all three are needed, they can be introduced to the fabric at the same time, as in bath dyeing. A hot water bath achieves the heat and moisture, and the fixing agents are then added to the bath. Sometimes it is advantageous or necessary to introduce these elements in separate steps. Often this is the case in hand painting or printing.

Usually the fixing agents and dissolved or liquid dyes are mixed together and applied by directly painting them onto the fabric, or they are thickened and screened on. Occasionally, before the dye touches the fabric, only the fixing agent is applied, or the fabric is soaked in the fixative for a short period and then dried. The fixing agent might be applied first because the dyes fix better or because the fixer would affect the thickener.

If the dyes need heat and moisture to fix, as with some fiber reactive, acid, and vat dyes, then dry the fabric with the applied dye. The fabric is then introduced to a steam chamber. The steam supplies both heat and moisture. Steam ironing is sometimes adequate for painted fabrics when resists and thickeners are not used, because they will melt into or scorch the fabric. Placing the fabric in a steamy bathroom will sometimes work, but more often a steamer is required.

A steamer can be set up at home in a large three- to five-gallon canning pan, either of enamel or stainless steel, or in a large Chinese basket steamer set in a shallow pan or wok. For protection against too much moisture, which will cause dyes to run, roll the fabric in clean unprinted newsprint. The paper should be longer and wider than the fabric. Fold a two-inch to three-inch heading of paper over the fabric and begin rolling fabric and paper together so that the fabric is not touching itself, or else the dye might transfer into other parts of it. Around this rolled bundle, wrap a layer of paper and a layer of towel or white felt (colored felt may bleed when steamed). Roll the outer layers firmly but not tightly. Fold the bundle into a canning rack or the basket of a steamer. It is important to keep the bundle away from the sides and lid where water collects. Put a small amount of water in the pan bottom and bring to a quick boil on the stove. Have the lid slightly askew to let out a little steam to cut down on condensation. Continue steaming for the recommended time. Fabric should be slightly moist and warm when unrolled. Industry uses large steamers in which the steam and heat can be controlled. Some commercial laundries or pleating houses offer a steaming service.

Fiber reactive dyes are constantly being improved to become more reactive at lower temperatures. Certain types need only moisture and time, both of which batching provides, and a few can fix at room temperature. When Cibacron F is printed on fabric, which is then batched and kept damp at least twenty-four hours, it will fix with very little loss of color when washed. The suggested method of batching prints is to let them dry until slightly damp, then roll them in plastic. This is one method, but other ways could be devised to keep the fabric damp.

Batching is an easier method of fixing than steaming, though steaming takes a shorter time and may be the only way to fix certain types of dye. Sometimes dyes for which steam fixing is recommended can be batched instead. Experiment by adding more or less fixing agents, particularly urea, or extending or shortening the batching time. Putting fabric in rolled plastic in a sunny window or a hot car might add enough heat to fix dyes.

Createx and other liquid fiber reactive dyes can be used in polychromatic printing if the urea is doubled in the chemical water recipe, and if the batching time is extended to forty-eight hours. There will be slightly more wash-off, particularly with turquoise, but the results are still worthwhile. If these dyes are painted straight onto the screen, they tend not to dry. Adding about one-quarter teaspoon water to one tablespoon dye assists in drying. Createx fiber reactive dyes seem to be slightly more concentrated in polychromatic printing than Cibacron F.

16

Washing Off

Summary

The objective is to thoroughly rinse out the print paste and excess dye from the printed fabric, after it has been batched.

The rinsing can be done in a bathtub or large sink. When the fabric has been rinsed, it is spun in a washing machine or rolled in towels until damp dry. Then it is ironed or hung up on a line to dry completely.

Sections to follow: Materials and Directions.

Materials

Rubber gloves.

Towels or washing machine. For removing excess moisture from printed fabric.

Have ready: 24-hour batched prints. Unroll from plastic; they can dry at this point without damaging the print, although it is not necessary that they dry for rinsing.

Sink or bathtub full of cold tap water.

Directions

Unroll printed fabric from plastic and immerse in bathtub or sink. Have enough water in the tub or sink so the fabric can float freely. If the fabric is too crowded, wash-off dye can spot it. Wearing rubber gloves, keep the fabric moving through the water for about five minutes. Drain the rinse water and refill the container. Continue rinsing in this manner until the water is clear and all sodium alginate is removed, and the fabric no longer feels slippery. Wring out as much water as possible by hand. NOTE: If it is difficult to remove the excess dye and the dyes bleed on the fabric, try using Synthrapol, a soapy scouring agent. (Refer to "Bath Dyeing," page 113.) Fill washing machine with cold water. Put fabric into water at rinse and spin dry cycle and run machine to end of cycle. Or, instead of using a washing machine, immediately after wringing out fabric, roll it in towels to remove excess moisture. Then hang it up to dry, or iron it. If silk and cotton are ironed while damp, wrinkles are easily removed. If completely dry, steam ironing will not usually have enough moisture to remove the wrinkles thoroughly. CAUTION: If the fabric stiffens and/or scorches easily, it means all the sodium alginate was not removed, and the rinsing process must be repeated. Some fabrics, including nan shan, shantung, and Shen's pongee silk, are inherently slightly stiff after printing and will soften with use.

17

Printing on Paper

Sections to follow: Materials; Directions; and Discussion.

Materials
Print screen. Refer to page 10.

Resist. Refer to page 33.

Fabric reactive dyes which dye cellulose fibers, Dr. Martin's or liquid watercolors, Caran d'ache watercolor crayons. The dyes work on paper as well as fabric. Dr. Martin's watercolors come in a large range of colors and are as potent as dyes and yield as many prints. Caran d'ache crayons can be marked directly on print screen to give a drawn image which will last up to four prints. Dr. Martin's watercolors and Caran d'ache crayons will wash out of fabric and are intended only for paper.

Paint brushes. Small, round, floppy Japanese or watercolor brushes for small detail areas, larger brushes for larger areas.

Mask-off screen. Refer to page 50.

Print surface. Smooth table top.

Materials for pulling print. Refer to page 69.

Paper. Choose an absorbent, medium to heavy paper such as heavier rice papers, construction paper, or watercolor papers with a smooth or slightly textured surface.

Masking tape.

Print paste. Refer to page 54.

Directions

The polychromatic process for printing on paper follows the same procedures as printing on fabrics, with two important exceptions. First, not only fiber reactive dyes can be used, but also Dr. Martin's and Caran d'ache crayons can be applied to the screen for a design; and second, the paper print does not need batching and fixing. The suggested color mediums fix immediately into paper.

The printing set-up can be the same as that for paper printing, or the sheets of paper can be taped down to a table and the screen moved. Refer to following discussion and to "Pulling Prints," page 69.

Discussion

Many fiber reactive dyes fix on cellulose, the major component of paper products. They work as well on paper as they do on fabric. Artists who make their own paper often use reactives to dye the pulp. In polychromatic printing dyes, Dr. Martin's Watercolors, and Caran d'ache crayons can be applied to the screen and transferred to paper with print paste.

Other color mediums may also be used in polychromatic paper printing, if they can be dissolved off the print screen with a solution or print paste, do not block the screen when applied, and adhere to paper. Refer to "Choosing Dyes," page 47, for further discussion of alternative color mediums.

The best papers for polychromatic printing are absorbent, medium-to-heavy weight, with little surface texture. The paper must be heavy enough to resist wrinkling and buckling, since the surface is covered with moisture in this particular printing method.

Two setups work for printing paper using the polychromatic method. In traditional paper printing, the screen is attached on the far side of the printing table by hinges with removable pins or by hinge clamps. The screen lifts, and the paper is placed beneath it. The squeegee is placed behind a thick ink or other color medium—spread across the far well. The squeegee is held firmly with both hands, usually at a 60 degree angle. Generally, the squeegee is pulled forward with as much downward pressure as possible, without bending the blade flat. The paper is replaced and the squeegeeing is repeated, sometimes in the opposite direction, away from the printer.

Screen and paper can also be set up as in traditional fabric printing. Instead of being placed under the hinged screen, the paper can be held to the table by masking tape, and the screen moved from one sheet to another. Moving the screen instead of the paper works easily in polychromatic printing, because a maximum of eight sheets of paper need to be taped down for one edition. Most of the paper surface is wet in polychromatic printing, creating a suction between screen and paper during squeegeeing. Taping the paper to the table helps hold it in place when the screen is lifted after printing. Refer to diagram, page 71.

Another approach to paper printing is off-contact printing. The hinged screen is raised slightly off the paper, about 1/8" to 1/4". This is done by raising the hinge above the table, perhaps by screwing it through a small piece of mat board. On the side opposite the hinges, a strip of mat board can be attached to level the frame. During printing, the screen contacts the paper only where the squeegee presses. The screen rises and releases the paper behind the squeegee.

Off-contact printing is not appropriate when fabric or paper has a tendency to stretch or shift. Off-contact printing can increase the chances of the printed image being blurred. In textile printing, total contact between the screen and fabric on a padded table (contact printing) is often necessary to make a clear print. Paper pick-up (refer to page 97) cannot be printed off-contact, because the screen shifts as the squeegee passes over, causing paper stencils to shift or buckle or ink to squirt under the stencil. Contact printing keeps the paper stencil suctioned to the screen.

18

Cleaning After Printing

Summary

The screens and equipment must be thoroughly washed to prevent any resist, dye, or print paste from affecting the next printing. Cleaning is done with a garden hose, spray nozzle, and cold water.

Sections to follow: Materials and Directions.

Materials

Garden hose with a spray nozzle.

Sponge and bucket of water.

Synthrapol.

To be cleaned after printing: print screen, squeegee, print paste pitcher and spoon.

Directions

Spray screen, squeegee, and print paste pitcher with water after printing, so they do not dry out. If dry, they will be more difficult to clean easily.

The best place to wash screens is outdoors. Lean the screens against a wall. Print paste can easily be sprayed off walls, if it sloshes. A concentrated stream of cold water from a garden hose will loosen the resist and print paste from the screen. Using warm to hot water doesn't speed up this process. Do not use a brush or scrubbing tool for cleaning, because they will raise fibers and damage the screen. In sticky spots, scratching with a fingernail will help loosen the resist. Be sure to remove all print paste from the cracks of the frame. Avoid using bleach, because it is difficult to get it completely out of the screen.

Even though the screen looks clear, resist may still be caught in its multi-filament threads. Soap up screen with a little Synthrapol on a sponge. Let screen soak for 5 minutes. Continue hosing the screen to clean out any resist that can't be seen. If the screen is not cleaned properly, leftover print paste may block it in the next printing, or the resist, though invisible, may appear as a concentrated line of dye in the next print.

Be sure to do a thorough cleaning. Plan to take 15-20 minutes for cleaning all equipment.

Let screen dry thoroughly before using it again. Spray the squeegee, plastic pitcher and spoon with water or clean in a sink. Be sure the print paste is diluted with water to prevent it from plugging the drain.

Wash off the plastic covering of the print surface using a sponge and water.

19

Care of Printing Equipment

Print Screen and Frame (1) No sharp objects that could cause the weave to shift or cut into the screen should ever come in contact with the screen. To clean the screen, do not use anything that will raise, cut or damage the screen fibers. (2) If at all possible, avoid cleaning with bleach, because it is difficult to rinse completely out of the screen. (3) Do not leave the screen too close to any heat source. Heat may melt the screen or bake the resist into it. (4) Do not get oil or grease on the screen, because that would result in the dye not painting evenly. (5) Have screen evenly supported at all times, with nothing pressing on it that might loosen the tension or push the frame out of shape. (6) Store the screen sideways in a protected area. (7) Do not leave frame in water for any length of time, because the wood will tend to bow. (8) Air-dry the screen as soon as possible after each use.

Print Surface (1) *Only* fabric stretching should be done on the print surface. It is easy to damage it by tearing and/or permanently indenting the plastic. (2) Store the print surface away from sharp objects and do not lean anything against it. (3) Do not get any oil or grease on the surface, because silk is highly absorbent and masking tape will not stick.

Squeegee (1) Keep the squeegee blade sharp at all times. NOTE: Sharpening may be done at a screen print supply outlet. Run hand down blade, checking for nicks; resharpen to remove them. (2) Do not let the squeegee sit in water, for it will warp. (3) Air-dry the squeegee immediately after use by hanging it by an eyelet in one end or by laying it flat in a protected area.

Paint brushes (1) Do not let brushes sit in water for any length of time. (2) After rinsing the dye from the brushes, squeeze them dry between fingers and form bristles into points before storing.

20
Problems and Solutions

1. *Problem: The resist will not flow evenly or is too thick to flow through the tjanting tool.* First, check to be sure the tjanting spout is not clogged. Tap point until it unclogs. If it is continually clogging, the resist may be lumpy. Strain it through a fine mesh strainer.

If the resist is too thick, try adding more water.

Be sure your tjanting tool is a large size, as smaller sizes will not allow the correct flow for an adequate line.

2. *Problem: Resist line is wider at ends where tjanting tool is lifted off or placed on the screen. A heavy resist application may form raised lumps when dry. This may cause inadequate contact and unclear prints.* There are two controlling factors for the resist. The consistency of the resist affects the flow through the tjanting spout. If the flow is too fast, add more glue and Inko resist and if it is too slow, add water. (Refer to "Resist," page 33.)

The other factor is the pace the tjanting tool is moved across the screen. When beginning and ending a resist line, move the tool quickly on and off the screen. Another solution may be to thicken the resist slightly to slow down the pace of moving the tool.

3. *Problem: The dye does not dry on the screen.* Check first to be sure your work space is not too damp. Try drying the screen outside, in the sun, or near a heater. (Refer to "Where to Work," page 25.)

Some types of dye will not dry on the screen. (Refer to "Discussion," page 48.)

4. *Problem: The dye bleeds into unwanted areas.* Check resist lines to be sure they are not too thin. Thin lines may be caused by drawing too quickly with the tjanting tool. Slowing your drawing speed allows more resist to flow out to form a wider line.

The tjanting tool hole is too small to form a wide line, or it may be clogged.

Check to be sure the dye is not taking an exceptionally long period to dry, since the resist lines can gradually dissolve into the dye if this happens.

5. *Problem: The dye is blocking many areas of the screen.* Check to be sure the dyes have not been painted too heavily onto the screen. (Refer to "Dye Application," page 41.)

Dyes dissolved in water may be old. They should be checked after two days. Note that some dyes may thicken even sooner.

Check to be sure there is enough water in the dye, because it may not have been measured correctly.

6. *Problem: Fabric does not stay stretched, because tape does not hold.* Check to be sure the tape is burnished or rubbed hard enough to make solid contact with the print surface or fabric.

The fabric must overlap at least ⅜" of tape width to prevent it from becoming untaped.

Check to be sure the print surface is dry and clean.

7. *Problem: Improper squeegeeing.* Check to be sure all your supplies for printing are organized from the beginning. When you are ready to pull the squeegee, your full attention is required. Before moving the squeegee, repeat to yourself three times: "Keep a steady, even speed at a 60 degree angle, with as much pressure as possible."

8. *Problem: The squeegee leaves a trail of dotted lines of print paste.* First check the squeegee's angle. If it is too upright, the print paste on the blade bottom will make contact with the screen. When this happens, quickly clean off the squeegee blade, wiping it against the frame or with a paper towel. Then run the squeegee across the screen with no print paste to pick up the trail. The correct pull angle is 60 degrees.

If the squeegee blade bottom was set into the print paste, instead of behind it in the well, there may be too much print paste on the bottom of the blade. In this case, even at a 60 degree angle, a trail will be made.

9. *Problem: Bubbles of unprinted areas appear on the print fabric.* Check to be sure the fabric was pulled tight enough and did not become untaped. Loose fabric cannot make good contact with the screen.

10. *Problem: The print is grainy and pale.* Check to be sure the fabric does not have too much texture or fuzz to make good contact with the screen. Sometimes more pressure on the squeegee will compensate.

Be sure the squeegee was not held at an improper angle or moved too quickly, preventing enough print paste from being forced through the screen. If this happened on the first print, the fabric has too much texture or fuzz. (Refer to "Fabric Sequence for Printing," page 61, for the best fabric selection.)

Check the print paste. It could be too thick, so that not enough of it is being pressed through the screen with the squeegee. Thin it by adding chemical water.

11. *Problem: The fabric does not make good contact with the sceen with one pull of the squeegee.* Refer to the "Problem/Solution," this page, for treatment of a grainy and pale print.

Check the print surface. There may not be enough padding, or the padding may be uneven, or the plastic may be buckling on the print surface.

If one part of the print is clear and another part not, it may be due to uneven pressure across the squeegee.

12. *Problem: The dye streaks across the print.* Check the print paste, because it does absorb some dye off the screen when squeegeed across. If there is enough print paste in the well, usually the absorbed dye does not get a chance to touch the screen. Sometimes with narrow wells, though, only enough print paste for one pull can be poured into the well. In this case, if the print paste has absorbed dye, clean the squeegee blade after each pull.

Too much dye may be painted on the screen or the dye was not dry before printing began, so that the print paste streaks it.

The pace of the moving squeegee across the screen may be too slow. This may allow the print paste time to absorb dye off the screen. In this case, speed up the squeegee.

The print paste may be too thin, thus absorbing the dye too quickly off the screen.

The dye may not have been adequately dissolved in water before it was added to the print paste, so a concentrated blob of dye streaked across the print.

13. *Problem: The print has a slightly dark line or a line which failed to print through the fabric.* Check to be sure there are no folds in the fabric. If there are, pull them out while stretching the fabric in preparation for printing or ironing out the fold.

Be sure there are no nicks in the squeegee blade.

14. *Problem: The print has light areas or spots where they were not intended.* A part of the fabric may have dried before it was rolled for batching. Dyes need moisture to set, or they will wash out, leaving a faint image.

Print paste may have dropped on the screen or may have been left on the screen by an improper pull of the squeegee. The drop of print paste will absorb the dye that is on the screen.

The plastic sheet for rolling prints may have been damp or had drops of water on it that absorbed some of the dye off the printed fabric. Always be sure that the plastic is dry and clean before using it.

The dry painted image on the screen may have been water spotted.

If bleach was ever used, it may still be on the screen or fabric.

15. *Problem: Specks of dye appear on the first print in an unpainted area, but do not appear on other prints.* Check to be sure the dye dust from clearing the screen or from dye powder was not on the screen in unpainted areas. Even though the screen looks clean, dye specks can be there.

16. *Problem: Dye specks on prints appear after the first print.* Check to be sure no dye dust is on the fabric, either from being rubbed off by sliding the dyed painted screen on the fabric or by dye powder dropping onto the fabric.

17. *Problem: The full number of prints cannot be obtained because the dye runs out too quickly.* Check to see if more pressure on the squeegee is needed and be sure to hold it at a 60 degree angle. This will release less dye on each print, leaving more dye on the screen for further prints.

Refer to "Fabric Sequence for Printing," page 59.

Print paste may be too thin, thus releasing more dye on each print.

Be sure to apply dye so that all holes of screen mesh are evenly filled. If the holes reopen quickly, paint on more dye. Do not use so much dye that it forms a puddle or a drop. This will cause the dye to block the screen.

If the dyes have been incorrectly measured or not thoroughly dissolved in water, they may not be at full concentration.

The age of the dyes might be the problem. Cibacron F and Procion dye powders have a shelf life of approximately two years. They gradually weaken in potency or may change color with age.

The squeegee blade could be dull, which could release too much print paste and dye from the screen. Keep the edge sharp at all times. Sharpen the blade at a screen print supply outlet.

18. *Problem: An unwanted image or dye appears over the original print.* Check to see if part of a wet print transferred dye onto the fabric when it was being moved or when it was in the plastic for batching. The fabric either folded upon itself or overlapped on another print and transferred dye.

The plastic for batching or the print surface may have dye left from previous prints.

19. *Problem: Dye from the print bleeds on fabric.* Check to be sure the fabric was rinsed enough. Try using Synthapol to aid in removing excess dye.

Too much water left in the fabric after rinsing can cause bleeding. Spin dry in a washer or wring out and roll in towels to remedy this problem. Hang the fabric up to dry or iron immediately after removing excess moisture.

Dye from the rinsed damp print may still transfer onto other areas of the fabric which touch each other for any length of time. Dry unfolded.

Dye may be unable to set into the fabric, because chemicals were incorrectly measured, batching time was shortened, there was a finish on the fabric that resisted the dye, or the fabric was not a 100 percent natural fiber.

A few fabrics will cause the dye to bleed slightly, giving fuzzy edges instead of hard clean lines in print.

20. *Problem: Dye does not fix on fabric or great amounts of dye come out in rinse water.* Check that the chemicals were measured correctly, the prints were batched damp and for a long enough period, and the dyes were not old.

The fabric might have had something on it or a finish which resisted the dye. "Prewashing" (page 65) may help.

If dye does not fix in bath dyeing, consider the above checkpoints (except for batching) and check the water temperature and length of time fabric was in the bath.

21. *Problem: Excessive dye and print paste left on print board after printed fabric is removed.*

The print paste was mixed too thin. Experiment with a thicker print paste consistency.

The fabric is too thin. Print on a canvas covered board with drop cloth. (Refer to "Print Surfaces," page 24.)

21
Other Ideas for Polychromatic Printing

There are many ways of applying dye and resist to the screen to get unusual effects. Polychromatic printing can be used with other screen print methods. There are ways of using the squeegee motion as a design element. Overprinting is another possibility. Following are some options which may be tried.

1. An atomizer or airbrush can be used to blow dyes onto the screen.

2. Water can be brushed on the screen, so that colors bleed into each other.

3. Straight lines can be applied quickly to the screen using masking tape. NOTE: The tape will not act as a resist to keep the dye from bleeding, so apply only after the dye is dry.

4. Resist can be mixed thicker or thinner to be applied not only with tjanting tool but also with paint brushes, a sponge, or by splattering and pouring, etc. If a large unprinted or resist area is desired, consider another method to block areas of the screen, preferably by the use of stencils, such as stencil blockout, profilm, photostencil or a photographic emulsion. In other words, dyes can be painted on a screen set up for another method of screen printing, as long as the blocking agent on the screen is not water-soluble. Otherwise, the dyes and print paste will dissolve the blocking agent or stencils. (Refer to "Discussion," page 38.)

5. Another method for blocking large areas of a screen is the paper pick-up method, sometimes called paper stencil. Cut paper in the desired shape and place it under the screen on the stretched fabric or paper for the first print. When squeegeed, the print paste will suction the paper shapes onto the screen for the duration of printing.

This pick-up method can be used in other ways. For surface textures, use glitter, confetti, punched-out circles, sewing threads, thin small leaves, etc., arranged on the fabric of the first print. Place the print screen over the fabric and textured materials. When squeegeed, the print paste will cause the textured material to adhere to the screen. Be sure any items placed under the screen are thin enough to make a clear image. If they are too thick, print paste will mount up around the item and the shapes will not make a sharp print or stick to the screen.

6. Several colors of print paste can be poured into the well and squeegeed across the screen at the same time. If there is a small print area blocked off on a large screen and a small squeegee is used, the squeegee can be pulled straight across the screen or, for a different surface pattern, the squeegee can be pulled at an angle or in a curving or waving motion.

7. It is also possible to overprint a design, either by shifting the same screen to a different position or by using a new screen. There are two methods for doing this: the first is to print over a damp print before it is batched. This method does have some restrictions. Damp printed fabric must stay pulled tight after the first printing. Some fabrics will buckle after printing, making it impossible for the screen to make good contact with the fabric a second time. Also, the fabric must absorb the printed dye and print paste quickly before the screen dries. If they lie on the fabric surface too long, the dye will come off on the back of the screen during overprinting, and transfer to the next prints. Heavy, absorbent fabrics will work best. Refer to page 60.

The second method of overprinting is to do two complete printing sessions. First, print one image onto the fabric, batch it, rinse it off, and iron it. Then restretch the fabric and print it again with the second design. Proceed as for a single print by batching, rinsing off, and ironing.

8. Several solutions can be coated on the print screen to minimize dye bleeding when painting on the screen. They are applied with a 1½ – 2" wide brush evenly saturating the screen mesh. No puddles or drops should form on the screen. Allow 15-30 minutes to dry, depending on the humidity. The most effective solution is one part print paste (the consistency for printing, with or without the urea and soda ash added) and two parts water. An alternative is to dissolve two tablespoons of table salt in ½ cup very hot water. This solution leaves a slightly jagged dye edge and slight texture in the solidly painted areas, but is still worth experimenting with.

9. The Inkodye resist can be used without glue. Add enough water to the Inkodye resist until the mixture is of a consistency to run evenly through the tjanting tool. Refer to "Resist Recipe" page 34. Apply in a heavy line with the tjanting tool and let it dry. Paint the dyes on and continue the poly-chromatic printing process. The difference is the resist line will eventually dissolve during the printing process and the print paste color will fill in the line. Also, liquid fiber reactive dye can be added to the Inko resist instead of water. The colored resist line will hold for the painting process and eventually break down in the printing process, leaving a colored line between the painted areas on the fabric. After printing, *carefully* roll damp fabric in plastic for batching (because resist is very wet).

Conclusion

I have been working with polychromatic printing since 1979. I have been able to earn a good income by designing, printing, and sewing jackets and scarves under the label "JOY." The polychromatic process is ideal for my small production line of limited editions and unique designs. However, when larger numbers of a design are needed, I generally use traditional methods of screen printing, which are set up to produce many more repeated images. I work with two print screens (each externally measuring 54" by 48"), using the method described on page 31 for printing garments. The screens are on hinges. The lightweight print surface trays are each registered under the screen by means of two thin, narrow boards tacked to the table at right angles to wedge the tray into place. My studio is a small space (300 square feet), which works well for this printing process. Less room is needed for printing panels than for traditional textile printing, which requires long tables to stretch yardage. Washing of equipment is done outdoors in the driveway with a garden hose.

I prefer Cibacron F dyes for printing and bath dyeing, because the colors mix true to the finished color of the dyed fabric and because they fix easily in batching. My total time for printing five jackets is approximately eight hours to design, print, and roll the fabric for batching. This is a relatively short time for a screen printing process.

The polychromatic method is a cross between printing and painting. In setting up this process, I selected from many aspects of both processes. In the directions I present one approach. After using this book as a guide, I hope the reader is convinced, as I am, that polychromatic printing offers an easy, flexible, direct, spontaneous notation of design for repetition, and permits a wide range of imaginative approaches.

APPENDIX A

Where to Buy Materials

Code	Retail Source	Location
A	Screen print supply outlets	Yellow Pages
B	Paper and packaging supply outlets	Yellow Pages
C	Plastic supply outlets	Yellow Pages
D	Fabric stores	Yellow Pages
E	Art supply stores	Yellow Pages
F	Hardware stores	Yellow Pages
G	Chemical supply outlets	Yellow Pages
H	PRO Chemical and Dye Inc.	P.O. Box 14 Somerset, MA 02726
I	Cerulean Blue, Ltd. (mail order)	P.O. Box 21168 Seattle, WA 98111
J	Dharma Trading Co.	P.O. Box 916 San Rafael, CA 94915 (800) 542-5227
K	Screen Process Supplies Mfg. Co. (mail order)	1199 East 12th Street Oakland, CA 94606
L	Exotic Silks (mail order)	1959 B Leghorn Mountain View, CA 94043
M	Test Fabrics (mail order)	P.O. Drawer O Middlesex, NJ 08846
N	Color Craft, Ltd. (mail order)	14 Airport Park Rd. Granby, CT 06026 (800) 243-2712
O	Rupert, Gibbon and Spider (mail order)	P.O. Box 425 Healdsburg, CA 95448
P	Basic Adhesive (mail order)	25 Knickerbocker Brooklyn, NY 11237
Q	Rubber Products Outlets	Yellow Pages

Materials	Source Code
PRINT SCREEN	
wooden canvas stretcher bars	E
sheer 100% polyester curtain fabric	D
staple gun	F
corrugated fasteners	F
wood for permanent frame	A, K
varnish	F
squeegee	A,E,K
PRINT SURFACE	
heavy gauge plastic	C,D,F
¾″ styrofoam or rigid insulation	C,F
corrugated cardboard	B
½″-¾″ Dacron batting	D
duct tape	E,F
hinge clamps	A
TRACING DESIGN ON SCREEN	
tracing paper, drawing paper	B,E
washable pen or pencil	D,E
RESIST	
Inkodye resist	K,I
Wilhold, Sobo or fabric white glues	D,F
squeeze bottle	F,H
tjanting tool	H,I,K,J,O

Materials	**Source Code**
DYE	
Cibacron F (see p. 104 for other dyes)	H,I
fine-particle face mask	F,J,H
small stiff brush	E
paint brushes	E,H,I,J
MASKING WELLS	
roll of heavy paper, brown paper tape, masking tape	A,B,E,F
permanent masking compount, Proseal	A
PRINT PASTE	
soda ash	G,H,I,J,N
urea	G,H,I,J,N
sodium alginate	
low-viscosity, high-solids	H,I,J,N,O
high-viscosity, low-solids	H,N,O
STRETCHING FABRICS	
cotton, silk, viscose rayon, linen fabrics	I,L,J,M,O
BATCHING	
large sheets of plastic	C,F
PRINTING ON PAPER	
fiber reactive dyes	H,I,J,N,O
Dr. Martin's or liquid watercolors	E
Caran d'ache watercolor crayons	E
papers	E

Materials	Source Code
DYE BATH	
fiber reactive dyes	
Cibacron F	H,I
Procion MX dye	H,I,J,O
Createx Liquid Cold Water Fiber Reactive Dyes	N
soda ash	G,H,I,J,N
plain salt	G or grocery store
MATERIALS FROM DISCUSSIONS	
heavy artist canvas for print surfaces	D,E
neoprene	Q
airbrush	E
stencil filler, glues, lacquer, varnish	A
photo stencil, photographic emulsion	A
stencil film, profilm	A
engrossing black	E
clear acetate	E
litho pencil and soft wax crayons	E
Kiton acid dye	H,I,J
Deka products	O,J
Inkodye products	K,I
Versatex	D,J
Createx products	N
wax for print table (Wax BA No. 116)	P
adhesive spray	A
Synthrapol	H,I,J,O

Complete List of Recipes

Resist
one part Inkodye resist
one part Wilhold or Sobo white glue

Dye
½ teaspoon dye powder
1 tablespoon water

Print Paste and Chemical Water
4 cups chemical water mixed from 2 tablespoons soda ash, 2 tablespoons
    urea, 4 cups water
2-3 tablespoons sodium alginate low-viscosity, high-solids,
    OR 4-5 tablespoons sodium alginate high-viscosity, low-solids

Dye bath for one pound of fabric (cotton, silk, viscose rayon)

LIGHT-MEDIUM COLORS	DARK COLORS
1½ cups plain salt	2 to 2½ cups plain salt
½ teaspoon to 1 tablespoon dye	2-4 tablespoons dye
3 gallons hot water from tap	3 gallons hot water from tap
⅓ cup soda ash	⅓ cup soda ash
1 quart hot water from tap	1 quart hot water from tap

APPENDIX C

Silk Organza and
Cotton Organdy Print Screen

Dyes painted on the suggested polyester screen will bleed. The resist is used to control the dye. But dyes painted on a print screen stretched with cotton organdy or silk organza fabrics do not bleed. This is similar to painting on paper. A hard edge between colors results, and the resist line to control bleeding is unnecessary. If bleeding is desired, wet the silk or cotton screen.

To print, using a silk or cotton screen, follow the same instructions as for polyester screen. The first print may have to be squeegeed more than once, because these are denser fabrics than the polyester. There will be one or two fewer prints, because the dyes will begin to react with the cotton or silk screens. This results also in a permanently dyed image in the screen that will not wash out. (NOTE: Do not use bleach because it will weaken the screen material.) This is usually a disadvantage, although it can be helpful if you want to reprint the same design.

Screens of these fabrics can also be used by watercolorists and painters who take a long time on one composition and can command a high price. For them, restretching a screen after one printing is not an unreasonable proposition.

APPENDIX D

Bath Dyeing

Summary
The objective is to obtain an overall even color on the fabric and to use the dye efficiently with the correct water temperature, and the correct proportion of dye to water, to chemicals, to fabric.

First, the dissolved dye is introduced into a salt water bath. The fabric is added and constantly moved through the bath for 5-15 minutes. It is then lifted from the dye bath, dissolved soda ash is added, the fabric is re-submerged, and constantly moved in the bath for 20-40 minutes. Fabric is then thoroughly rinsed in cold water and spun dry or wrung out and rolled in towels to remove the excess moisture. As a final step, the fabric is either ironed, machine dried, or hung on a clothesline to dry.

Sections to follow: Materials; Recipe; Directions; Test Color of Dye Bath; Receptivity of Fabric to Dye; Where to Dye; and Discussion.

Materials
Fiber reactive dyes. Cibacron F, Procion MX or Createx reactive dyes.

5-gallon container. A shallow 15"×15"×8" stainless steel, enamel or plastic container. NOTE: Plastic is the easiest to use.

Rubber gloves.

Timer.

8-oz. container for mixing dye. Glass, stainless steel, or plastic.

Spoon. For mixing dye.

Blender. To dissolve thoroughly four tablespoons of dye.

Set of measuring spoons or small gram scales. For measuring dye. Gram scales are more accurate.

Washing machine (on rinse cycle) or towels.

Plastic clothespins. NOTE: Wooden pins will absorb dye and leave marks on fabric.

Salt. Plain salt.

Soda ash.

One pound cotton, silk, linen, viscose rayon fabric.

Sponge. Used only for dye clean-up.

Recipe for dye bath for one pound fabric (cotton, silk, viscose rayon, linen)

LIGHT-MEDIUM COLORS
1½ cups plain salt
½ teaspoon to 1 tablespoon dye
3 gallons hot water from tap
  (use warm water around 100
  degrees for Procion)
⅓ cup soda ash
1 quart hot water from tap

DARK COLORS
2-2½ cups plain salt
2-4 tablespoons dye
3 gallons hot water from tap
⅓ cup soda ash
1 quart hot water from tap

Directions

It is essential to be organized and work fast. The fabric to be dyed should already have been weighed and cut. Dissolve measured dye in a small amount of hot water in a small jar or blender. Dissolve the soda ash in one quart of hot water. Measure the salt and pour into five-gallon container.

Now pour three gallons of the hottest tap water available into a five-gallon container. At same time, dissolve the salt by stirring water with rubber-gloved hands. Add the dye and stir thoroughly. Immediately add the fabric. Work quickly to prevent fabric from streaking. Open up the entire length of fabric, making sure the dye has thoroughly saturated it. Continue opening the fabric, from selvedge to selvedge and from one end to the other, allowing five minutes for light colors and ten to fifteen minutes for medium to dark colors.

With one hand, lift the fabric out of the dye bath, and with the other hand, pour the dissolved soda ash into the bath, and mix it into the bath. Return the fabric to the dye bath. This is another critical point to prevent streaking the fabric, so work fast to open the fabric from end to end. Continue doing this at a slower pace, allowing 20 minutes for light to medium colors and 30-40 minutes for medium to dark colors.

To rinse, discard the dye from the container and squeeze as much dye out of the fabric as possible. Fill the container with cold water, opening the fabric up from end to end. Discard the rinse water, and refill the container again with cold water. Repeat this rinsing process 4-5 times, or until the water runs almost clear. Be sure to remove all dye from the fabric, since any dye left can cause streaks. Run the fabric through the rinse cycle of a washing machine, so it will be spun dry. Or wring out as much water as possible by hand and roll it in towels to dry further. NOTE: If excess dye is difficult to remove, try using Synthapol, a scouring agent, in the rinse. Refer to discussion, page 113. Either dry the fabric in the dryer (be sure the fabric is not twisted), or hang it on the clothesline, using plastic clothespins.

Iron out the wrinkles thoroughly while the fabric is still damp. Often steam ironing will not remove all wrinkles, and some steam irons can leak drops of water, which often leave a water spot. If water should get on the fabric, soak it again in cold water immediately and repeat the rinse process.

When damp ironing, keep the iron moving at all times, so a hard line does not develop between dry and damp areas of the fabric. This can cause a dye line to show. Ironing is not necessary for setting the dyes. The best way to store fabric yardage which has been dyed is by rolling it, rather than folding it.

Test Colors of Dye Bath

Every brand of dye, paint, and ink has its own special color language. As you use the various brands, you will develop a memory for the color mixing that works with each type.

Test dye colors in two ways: (1) After dissolving the dye in a small jar, dilute a few drops of dye in water. This will give an approximate idea of the color you are heading towards, although some colors will fix into fabric quickly and some, more slowly. This test method doesn't allow for these differences, nor does it show the strength of color intensity. (2) The following method is more accurate but must be done quickly, because the dye bath is cooling. Have a few 2″ squares of fabric ready, each held by a plastic clothespin. Clothespins will help locate a fabric square if it is lost in the dye bath. As soon as the dye is added to the hot water and salt bath, hold the clothespin and quickly swish the fabric square through dye water. The movement helps the dye penetrate the fabric faster. Remove from the dye bath after about one minute. This test will give a fairly accurate idea of the dye color, although, keep in mind, the color intensity will lighten when dry. If another color needs to be added, do so quickly and test again with a new fabric square. If the color is completely wrong, mix another dye bath and retest the color with new fabric swatches.

Adding more dye to overpower a color already present often is a waste of dye. Adding dye once the actual fabric is in the bath will usually not change the color very much. If the latter is done, be sure to remove the fabric from the bath, add the dye, mix, and reintroduce fabric to the bath. If attempting to duplicate the color of a previously dyed piece of fabric, wet the fabric so it will compare to the wet 2″ square test sample. Sometimes holding the two fabrics up to a window to let light shine through will show more clearly any color differences.

It is very difficult to reproduce accurate colors using dye recipes, even if scales are used to weigh and measure dyes accurately. There are many variables affecting dyes: age, concentration of dye in bath water, water temperature, and timing.

As your color knowledge increases, you will find it easier to analyze and select base dyes to mix your colors. On the most professional level, a dye colorist working in the textile industry knows the dyes so well, he or she can decide the color make-up and proportions without prior testing.

Receptivity of Fabric to Dye

Some fabrics are more receptive to dye than others. Test "new" fabrics by dyeing a small sample in a dye bath along with a fabric known to be receptive. If the new fabric dyes pale in comparison, you may find it helpful to add dye. However, don't depend on this. There is no guarantee that darkening the color will always work. Experimentation is still best.

Fabrics used for bath dyeing should have no finishes or sizing on them. This is more critical in bath dyeing than in the batching process, since the dye has less time in the dye bath to penetrate the fabric. Fabrics with sizing or finishes will be the hardest to penetrate in a short amount of time.

MOST RECEPTIVE FABRICS	LESS RECEPTIVE FABRICS
silk satin	pongee silks
silk broadcloth	some cottons
raw silk or silk noil	linen
spun silk	
China silk	
jacquard silk	
charmeuse	
crepe de chine	
viscose rayon	
some cottons	

Where to Dye

An old laundry room is the perfect spot. Choose space where dye splashes and stains will not harm walls or counters, although dye does wash off formica, enamel paint and floor tiles. An enamel bathtub also works well, because splashes hit tub sides but not walls and can be easily washed off. However, a tub does require kneeling, which can be hard on the back.

In addition, the dye area must have running water (hot and cold) and a sink or tub with a drain. Place the five-gallon plastic container for the dye bath in the sink or tub, because a tub or sink absorbs the heat from water more quickly than plastic. It is important to keep dye bath warm as long as possible.

Discussion

In addition to fiber reactive dye, the dye bath ingredients are water, salt, and soda ash. The quantity of dry goods determines the amount of water. There must be enough water to distribute the dye evenly, but not so much that the dye concentration is lost.

The dye bath directions recommend using a plastic tub. This allows for optimum control and less dye wastage when dyeing small amounts of fabric. However, two or more pounds can be difficult to manage in a tub. Use a washing machine if more than two pounds are to be dyed. Refer to Appendix F, page 116.

For most cold fiber reactive dyes, the optimum fixing temperature recommended by the manufacturer is in the range of 95 to 120 degrees F. Dyes will set faster at higher temperatures and bring out the color depth.

First, dye and salt are dissolved in water. The fabric is added to this bath. Constant movement of the fabric in the salt bath disperses the dye evenly in the fabric. Next, soda ash is added to fix the dye in the fabric. The longer the fabric is in the dye bath before the soda ash is added, the more the dye can react with fabric fibers.

Very pale pastel colors use small amounts of dye, approximately one to two teaspoons. Streaking can occur more easily when there is less dye to spread evenly over the fabric, and streaking will show more on light colors than on dark colors. To slow the absorption of dye onto the fabric, so that the dye has time to distribute evenly, use colder water and move the fabric in a water and dye bath, without salt, for ten minutes. Lift out the fabric. Add the salt dissolved in three cups of warm water and resubmerge the fabric. Move the fabric in this bath for ten minutes, then lift out the fabric. Add the dissolved soda ash. Return the fabric to the bath and move for twenty minutes. Then rinse.

The final step, rinsing, is critical with reactive dyes. Rinsing must be extremely thorough. Be sure to rinse the dyed fabric until the rinse water runs clear or streaking can occur. Synthrapol may be used to rinse out remaining dye from a color difficult to remove, such as turquoise, or when a concentrated dye bath was used to produce an extremely deep shade.

When using Synthrapol, first rinse the fabric one or two times to remove most of the dye. Then fill another rinse bath with hot water and add to the rinse water one tablespoon of Synthrapol per pound of fabric. Put the fabric into this solution and agitate for about ten minutes. Rinse fabric again to remove Synthrapol and remaining dye, until the water runs almost clear. Follow instructions for drying and ironing on page 109.

If the dry, dyed fabric has streaks along the seams or edges, the excess dye was not completely removed. A mottled appearance may indicate that the fabric was not agitated enough or the dye and/or soda ash were unevenly distributed in the dye bath. Light spots showing occasionally through the fabric may indicate that the soda ash was not completely dissolved. Dye powder not thoroughly dissolved leaves dark, concentrated spots.

Color Mixing

There are seven base dye colors from which all other dye colors are mixed. They are:

yellow (lemon yellow)	*scarlet*	*blue*
golden yellow (yellow orange)	*fuschia**	*navy*
		turquoise**

*red is usually a combination of fuschia and scarlet

**(not available in Cibacron F)

In addition to these seven colors, black and brown can be used as base colors, although they, too, are usually mixed from the seven base colors.

Everyone, including the dye manufacturer, has his or her own vision of what a color truly looks like. To some eyes, for example, a brown dye might look too orange or red and need more blue added.

Navy is usually a very potent dye, staying dark longer through the printing process than any other color. It is usually the basis for black. Black dyes often lean towards colors other than gray. Some are blue-blacks or green-blacks, or on different fibers, a black will have a different cast entirely. To obtain a gray from a black, or to make it a truer black, there is a logical method to follow once a few basics are learned.

Basics in Color Mixing

1. Complements (colors opposite each other on the color wheel) give a gray cast when properly mixed. To make a black a more true black, if it is a green-black, add just a touch of red dye. Use the proportions, one teaspoon black dye to one-eighth teaspoon red dye.

2. When mixing colors, always begin with the lighter color. When mixing green, start with yellow and slowly add blue to get the shade of green desired.

3. To obtain the brightest dye color, start mixing with the brightest primary colors. Example: to get purple, use fuschia and turquoise, instead of red or scarlet and navy or blue.

4. To mix a deep color, choose the darker of the primary colors: For example, if a deep midnight blue or teal is wanted, instead of choosing turquoise and yellow and making a bright blue-green, use navy and golden yellow and obtain a darker, deeper shade of green-blue. Adding the opposite color to a color often dulls it, but often does not darken it. The best way to dull and darken a color is to add black.

5. To deepen instead of darkening or dulling a bright color, add a very small amount of blue or navy. Adding a *little* blue to scarlet makes it a richer hue.

6. There is no white in dyes, only in pigments. To lighten a color and make it close to a pastel, use less concentrated dye, by diluting it with water. Lavender, pink and tan are lighter diluted versions of purple, fuschia and brown.

Bath Dyeing in the Washing Machine

This washing machine technique cannot be done at a laundromat, as you need to have control over the machine's cycles. An old non-automatic machine is great if you can find one, as there is no chance of accidently dumping the dye water too soon.

Washing machine dyeing yields very professional results. Dyes go on evenly for large batches more easily than dyeing in garbage pails or big buckets. It's great for dyeing 2-3 dozen T-shirts, old sheets, and fabrics by the yard.

1. Run goods through regular wash cycle and rinse cycle using detergent. Remove goods.

2. Fill machine full of *hot* water (i.e., shut off cold tap input). Use full machine for dyeing 5-8 pounds, ½ machine for dyeing 2-4 pounds.

3. Add 1 pound of salt for half machine load, 3 pounds of salt for full load.

4. Make a paste of ½-1 ounce of dye powder for ½ load or 1-1½ ounces for full load. Add salt slowly while machine is agitating. Then slowly add dissolved dye paste (dilute with a cup or two of water). Place goods in the washer.

5. Agitate the machine with just the salt and dye for 10 minutes.

6. Turn machine back to beginning of agitation cycle again and *slowly* add ½ cup of soda ash for ½ load, or full cup for full load. Continue agitating after adding for 10 minutes.

NOTE: Be careful at this point to keep an eye on the machine or it will drain and all your dye will go down the drain!

7. Shut off machine for 15 minutes or so, then agitate for 5-10 minutes. Shut machine off again for 15 minutes, then agitate again for completion of cycle. Let the machine empty the dye solution out and run through a rinse cycle.

8. Run through one complete wash cycle and use detergent. For extra deep colors you may wish to do two complete wash-rinse cycles.

Dyed items can then be dried in dryer or hung on clothesline. If streaks appear at seams and edges of fabric after drying, you have not washed out the excess dye well enough. When using your machine to completely wash and rinse the dyed items, you will also be thoroughly cleaning the machine and will not need to worry about washing regular clothes.

"Bath Dyeing in the Washing Machine"
by permission of Susan C. Druding

GLOSSARY

Afterimage - a faint image from a previous printing.

Airbrush - a device for spraying dyes or paints, operated by compressed air.

Batching - a process of fixing dye onto fabric by keeping the fabric damp at room temperature for twenty-four hours or longer.

Bath dyeing - a method of dyeing a fabric one even color in a bath.

Blocked screen - screen mesh holes clogged with dried resist or dye or print paste.

Blocking agent - a substance or material used for blocking the print screen mesh to prevent the squeegeed print paste, ink, etc., from passing through the screen.

Block-out - a liquid used to block the print screen mesh to prevent the squeegeed substance from passing through it.

Cellulose fiber - a fiber from plant material such as flax for linen, wood pulp for rayon, or cotton.

Cibacron F - a type of fiber reactive dye, also named Fibracron Dye.

Contact - the connection between the screen and fabric, caused by the pressure of the squeegee pulled across the screen surface.

Deposit - the substance (print paste, etc.) left on the printed surface (paper, fabric, etc.) after squeegeeing.

Dry goods - textiles (fabric yardage, clothing, etc.)

Edition - print pulled from one screen, or run.

Fiber reactive dye - a dye class or type that forms a very strong chemical bond with the fiber. Cibacron F and Procion are dyes in this class.

Fixing or fixation of dye - the permanent setting of the dye into the fibers.

Fixing agent or fixer - a chemical used to set permanently the dye into the fibers.

Grain of fabric - the direction of the lengthwise woven threads of the fabric.

Internal measurement of screen - measurements from the inside edge of the frame bars.

Mesh of screen or screen mesh - the open spaces between the threads of the fabric pulled over the frame.

Monoprinting - an edition of one print.

Monofilament - single strand forming a thread.

Overprint - printing on top of previously printed fabric or paper.

Paper pick-up - a method of screen printing where stencils of paper or thin items are placed under the screen on the first piece (of paper or fabric) to be printed. When the squeegee passes over the screen, the squeegeed substance suctions the items onto it for the rest of the printing session, creating a stencil.

Polychromatic screen printing - process of applying dye colors to a print screen, letting them dry, then transferring the colors to fabric or paper by squeegeeing print paste across the screen. No color registration is required. Usually editions are limited to 5-8 prints.

Print paste - the substance, squeegeed across the screen, containing thickener, water, dye, and sometimes the fixing agent.

Print area - the design area of the screen.

Print screen - a wooden or metal frame over which an open mesh fabric is stretched for screen printing. Refer also to "Screen Printing."

Procion dye - a type of fiber reactive dye.

Protein fiber - fibers from animal hairs or protein sources, such as wool from sheep and silk from the silkworm cocoon.

Pulling a print - the movement of pulling or moving the squeegee across the print screen (also called squeegeeing).

Reactives - short for fiber reactive dyes.

Registration - the lining up of a sequence of colors and the print frame to print one design.

Resist - the blocking medium applied to the print screen to prevent dye or print paste from bleeding into unprinted areas of the design.

Run - see *Edition.*

Selvedge edge - the two parallel bound edges running the fabric length.

Screen printing - a printing method where a colored medium (inks, print paste, etc.) is forced through an open mesh fabric using a squeegee.

Squeegee - a flat blade of rubber or other pliable material set in a wooden handle.

Squeegeed substance - any material forced through the screen by the squeegee, such as print paste or inks.

Squeegeeing - the act of pulling the squeegee across the screen surface.

Stencil - a medium (photographic emulsion, etc.) used to block the screen to keep color from areas of the design.

Thickener - an agent used for thickening liquid (usually water) in print paste. Sodium alginate is a thickener.

Tjanting tool - a Javanese tool used for painting with hot wax in batik designs. A small metal bowl with a narrow spout is attached to a wooden handle.

Toosh - solvent-soluble blocking agent.

Tusche - water-soluble blocking agent.

Viscosity - resistance of a substance to flow.

Washing out - washing or rinsing the excess dye and/or thickener from the fabric.

Washoff - the excess dye rinsed from the fabric.

Wells - the masked border on four sides of the printable screen area which are used to hold the print paste and the squeegee away from the print after each print pull.

INDEX

A

acetic acid, 45, 46
acid donor, 57
acid dye, 45-46, 57, 78
   thickener, 57
adhesive spray, 68, 74, 104
afterimage, 17, 118
airbrush, 32, 49, 96, 118
alkaline fixative, 45, 46, 48

B

backcloth, 24
batching, 7, 25, 58, 60, 65, 75-78, 79,
   92, 94, 111, 118
bath dyeing, 58, 65, 78, 107-113, 118
   amount of water, 108, 112
   color testing, 110-111
   concentration, 112
   problems, 94-95, 113
   receptive fabrics, 111
   recipe, 105, 108
   rinsing, 109, 113
   streaking, 109, 113
   temperature, 108, 112
binder for ink, 45, 57
bleach, 17, 38, 87, 106

blockage or blocked screen or
   clogging, 56-57, 118
   see also dye, blocking screen
blocking agents, 17, 37-39, 96, 118
   directly applied, 38, 39
   solvent-soluble, 38
   water-soluble, 38-39, 96
block-out or stencil block-out, 38, 96,
   104, 118

C

canvas print surface, 24, 68, 104
cellulose fiber or fabric, 45, 46, 47,
   62, 118
chemical water, 54, 55, 56, 105
Cibacron F, 40, 47, 79, 99, 103, 120
   recipe, 41, 105
   see also dye
Ciba Vat Dye, 46, 104
color, for dye mixing,
   base or primary colors, 3, 114, 115
   black, 114, 115
   duplicating, 110-111
   mixing, 114, 115
   testing, 110-111
   see also turquoise; white
color fastness, 47

contact, *see* print screen
contact printing, 84
cotton, 60, 62, 63, 64, 65, 103, 111
   batiste, 64
   broadcloth, 60, 64
   canvas, 24, 60, 64
   corduroy, 61, 64
   lawn, 60, 64
   muslin, 24, 60, 64
   poplin, 60, 64
   organdy, 64, 106
   sailcloth, 64
   sateen, 60, 63
   terry, 64
   voile, 64
   see also screen fabric, cotton
      organdy
Createx Liquid Cold Water Fiber
   Reactive Dye, 47, 48, 58, 79, 104
Createx textile fiber pigments, 45, 104
crepe fabric, printing, 68
Cushing dye, 46

D

Deka Iron-on Transfer Paints,
   46, 104
Dekaprint, 45, 104
Deka "Series L", 46, 104
deposit, 17, 18, 58, 74, 118
design for print, 5-6, 27, 30-31
   apply to screen, 28
   continuous repeat, 23, 30
   formats, 30-31
   isolated image, 29, 31
   reverse, 28, 30
Disperse Dye, 46, 104

disperse dyes, 46
   thickener, 57
dye, 26, 40-49
   adding to print paste, 56
   application and concentration, 6,
      37, 41-43, 48-49, 93
   bleeding, 6, 28, 37, 43, 56, 90, 94
   blocking screen, 17, 26, 40,
      43-45, 48, 70, 90, 93
   characteristics, 47-48
   colors, *see* color
   color fastness, 47
   diluting, 43
   drying on screen, 42, 48, 89-90
   dust or specks, 44, 48, 70, 93
   exhaust, 59, 73
   liquid, 41, 47, 48
   penetration, 60, 65
   powder, 40, 93, 113
   problems, 89-90, 92, 93, 94
   precautions, 41, 43, 47
   recipe, 41, 48, 105
   rinsing or wash off, 7, 47, 80-81,
      92, 109, 113
   shading, 32, 48-49
   storing, 40, 47
   streaks in dyeing, 109
   streaks in printing, 92
   unwanted bleeding, 90, 94
   see also types of dyes;
      bath dyeing
dye bath, *see* bath dyeing
dye dust or specks, 44, 48, 70, 93

E

edition, 23, 30, 119
extender for ink, 45, 57

F

fabric,
    cellulose, 45, 46, 47, 62
    color for printing, 59
    dye penetration, 60, 65, 66
    finishes, 59, 65
    natural, 59-60, 62
    protein, 45, 46, 47, 62
    selvedge, 12, 63, 120
    synthetic, 45, 46, 62, 65
    see also receptive fabrics; ironing;
        print fabric, absorbent; weaves
fabric printing, conventional, 23, 30,
    37-39, 99
fiber reactive dyes, 6, 40, 46-48, 78,
    79, 83, 104, 112, 119
filaments, 62, 63
fix dye, 7, 57, 58, 62, 65, 78-79, 119
    steam setting, 46, 57, 58, 78-79
    temperature, 46-47, 78, 79, 112
    see also batching
fillers or stencil fillers, 38
fixing agents, 45, 57-58, 78, 79, 119
    acid, acetic, 45, 46
    alkaline, 45, 46, 48
    application of, 54, 57, 78-79
    baking soda, 46, 58
    ink, 45, 65
    problems, 94-95
    soda ash, 46, 48, 54, 55, 58, 103,
        112, 113
    TSP, 46, 58
fixing inks, 45
frame, see print screen, frame

G

garment, printing fabric, 1, 31, 65, 99
    see also fabric printing

H

halftone positive, 39
hand-cut stencils, 38
hand painting on fabric, 37, 65, 78
hinge clamps, 23, 71, 83, 102

I

Inkodye resist, 25, 33, 34, 89, 102
inks, 38, 39, 45, 57, 65, 68, 74
Inko-Tex, 45, 104
ironing, 78, 81, 92, 109-110
    steam, 109
    stiffening or scorching, 81
isolated image, 29, 31

L

lacquer-base film, 38
lightweight fabric printing, 74
    see also scarf printing
lightweight print board, see print
    surface
linen, 60, 62, 103, 111

M

masking compound, 50, 51-53, 103
masking wells, see wells
momme (mm), 60, 61

monagum thickener, 57
monofilament, 119
multifilament, 62

N

negative image, 38
neoprene, 24, 68, 104
nylon, 17, 62

O

off-contact printing, 84
oilcloth, 19-20, 24, 68
overprinting, 31, 97-98, 119

P

paint brushes, 41, 88, 103
paper for printing, 17, 82, 83, 103
    buckling, 83
paper pick-up or paper stencils, 84,
    97, 119
paper printing,
    conventional, 17, 23, 38-39, 68,
        83-84, 99
    polychromatic, 82-84
photo emulsion or stencil, 38, 39, 96,
    104
pigment, 45
polychromatic printing, maximum
    prints, 18, 59
positive image, 39
preshrinking, 65
prewashing, 65, 95

print area, 12, 15, 27, 28, 119
print board, *see* print surface
print fabric,
    absorbent, 59, 60
    categories, 30, 59-61
    fuzz, 60, 91, 94
    pinning, 24, 68
    problems, 91-95
    receptive, 111
    redampen, 78
    sequence, 59-61
    size, 66
    stretching, 6, 7, 66-68, 90
    texture, 59, 60, 66, 74
    types, 59-61, 66
    unsatisfactory, 61
    see also fabric; ironing, wash off
print paste, 6, 31, 54-58, 69, 70, 72,
        73, 74, 78, 91, 92, 120
    adding dye, 56, 92
    consistency, 54, 55-57, 92, 93
    deposit, 17, 18, 58, 74, 118
    function, 6, 54, 56-57, 69, 73
    recipe, 55-56, 105
print screen,
    blocked, 17, 41, 48, 118
    cleaning, care, 28, 85-86, 87
    construction, 5, 10, 12-16
    contact, 6, 18, 59, 60, 68, 72, 73,
        84, 91-92, 118
    exhausting, 59, 73
    external size, 12, 15
    frame, 10, 12, 13, 15, 16, 20-21,
        66, 102
    internal size, 12, 15, 119
    painting, *see* dye, application

permanent, 10, 13, 16, 102
set-up for printing, 20-21, 23, 70, 71, 83-84
size, 5, 10, 11-12, 20-21, 59, 60, 61
temporary screen, 10, 16, 102
see also design; screen fabric
print surface,
adhesive, 68, 74
canvas, 24, 68
care and cleaning, 24, 66, 86, 87
characteristic, 19, 23, 68
neoprene, 24, 68, 104
padding, 5, 19, 21, 23, 84, 91
set-up for printing, 19, 20-21, 71
size, 20-21
tacky, 68
unpadded, hard, 23, 74
wax, 68, 104
printing,
crepe, 68
lightweight fabrics, 74
scarves, 68
textured fabric, 17, 59, 66, 74
T-shirts, 68, 74
Procion dye, 40, 47, 104, 120
Proseal, 50, 103
see also masking compound
pulling prints, 59, 69, 70-74, 83-84
problems, 90-91

R

rayon, viscose, 60, 62, 65, 103
challis, 60, 64
satin, 60, 64

receptive fabrics to dye, 111
registration, 1, 23, 30, 120
resist, 37-38, 120
application, 6, 33, 34-36, 90, 96
characteristic, 37
consistency and flow, 25, 34, 37, 89
design element, 25, 28, 31, 96
drying, 25, 26, 33, 36
lumps, 34, 89
problems, 83, 89
recipe, 25, 34, 105
resist stencils, 38, 39
reverse image, 30, 32
Rit, 46

S

salt, 108, 109, 110, 112-113
scarf printing, 68
scouring agent, *see* Synthrapol
screen fabric or mesh, 10, 17, 28, 119
cotton organdy, 17, 31-32, 37, 106
cut size, 11, 12
mesh size, 11, 17, 39
nylon, 17
polyester, 5, 11, 17, 25, 102
silk organza, 17, 31-32, 37, 106
stretching, 12-13, 14
tooth, 17

silk, 60, 62-63, 64, 65, 103
  boucle, 64
  broadcloth, 60, 64, 111
  charmeuse, 60, 63, 111
  chiffon, 64
  China silk, 60, 64
  crepe, 62, 68, 111
  degummed, 62-63
  douppioni, 62
  georgette, 64
  grograin, 64
  gum, 62
  jacquard, 111
  nan shen pongee, 60, 64, 81
  noil, 60, 62, 64, 111
  organza, 64, 106
  pongee, 60, 64, 111
  raw, 62, 64
  satin 60, 111
  shantung pongee, 60, 64, 81
  Shen's pongee, 60, 81
  spun, 60, 62, 111
  taffeta, 60, 64
  Thai, 60
  tussah, 62, 64
  wild, 62
soda ash, *see* fixing agent
sodium alginate, 54, 55, 56-58, 81,
  103
  see also print paste; thickener
solids content, 57
squeegee and squeegeeing, 10, 11,
  17-18
  angle, 70, 73, 91, 93
  blade, 11, 17-18, 72, 87, 91, 92
  care for, 87
  handle, 72
  pace, 72, 74, 92

polyurethane, 18
pressure, 10, 11-12, 18, 59, 72,
  73, 91, 92, 93
problems, 90-91, 92, 93
rhythm, 74
rubber, 11, 18
sharpening, 87, 94
size, 15, 16
staple, of fiber, 62, 63
steam setting, 46, 57, 58, 78-79, 109
stencils, 17, 38, 39, 96, 104, 121
  block-out, 38, 96
  filler, 38
  hand-cut, 38
Synthrapol, 81, 94, 104, 109, 113

T

tacky print surface, 68
textile printing, conventional, 23, 30,
  38-39, 99
thickener, 56-58, 121
  see also sodium alginate
Tintex, 46
tjanting tool, 6, 33, 34-36, 37, 89, 90,
  102, 121
  pace for drawing, 89, 90
tooshes, 38, 121
tooth, 17
T-shirt printing, 68, 74
tusches, 38, 121
turquoise, 113, 114, 115

U

urea, 48, 58, 79, 103

V

vat dyes, 46, 78
velvet, 61, 64
velveteen, 64
Versatex, 45, 104
viscose rayon, *see* rayon
viscosity, 57, 121

W

washing machine dyeing, 112,
   116-117
wash off, 7, 47, 80-81, 92, 109, 121
washing soda, 54, *see also* soda ash
water-based inks, 45
water-soluble blocking agents, 38-39
water soluble films, 38
wax print surface, 68, 104
weaves, 63-64
   satin, 63
   tabby or plain, 63, 64
wells, 5, 15, 35, 43, 50-53, 70, 121
   masking, 6, 31, 50-53
   permanent, 35, 43, 51-52
   size, 12, 27-28
   temporary, 50-51, 52
white, 45, 115